Morecambe & Wise

To Wendy's Dad,
from Gilly's hubbie

B'3 of Love

Ted

First published in Great Britain in 1997 by Chameleon Books
an imprint of André Deutsch Ltd
106 Great Russell Street
London WC1B 3LJ

André Deutsch Ltd is a subsidiary of VCI plc.

10 9 8 7 6 5 4 3 2 1

Designed by William Harvey.

Printed and bound in Italy by Officine Grafiche DeAgostini.

A catalogue record for this book is available from the British Library
ISBN 0 233 99175 1

Morecambe & Wise

You Can't See The Join

by Jeremy Novick

For my father, who also had it snatched away

And ... as ever, to Gilly, Elly, Maxwell C Wolf and Lexa – perfectly formed, everything a boy could wish for.
And to Cissi, who was there at the beginning and there at the end, a sweetie who's finally grown into her skin.

So to the thanks. A huge thank you to Joan Morecambe who was as kind as kind can be, and another big thank you to Gary Morecambe who was helpful, and kind and sweet. I thought they'd be protective of the memory, or bored of talking about it or something in between. But they weren't. They were generous and kind and sweet. Really, it was the icing on the cake.
Also, a big thanks to Ernest Maxin, Angela Rippon, Doreen Wise, and the estate of Dennis Holman, whose Eric & Ernie, The autobiography of Morecambe & Wise was of invaluable assistance in the writing of this book. Plus, thanks to Nigel, Mal and John.

But most of all, to my mother.

Like Joan and Ernie, she knows what it's like.

FOR REASONS THAT aren't relevant here – it's a long story – I was walking across the brow of a mountain in Nepal a few years ago with my friend Cissi, a 22-year-old Swedish woman.

It was a lovely mountain, but we had a lot of time on our hands and Cissi, bless her, loves to talk. The subject of TV programmes we used to watch as kids came up. Cissi told me about a bull called Ferdinand who used to sit underneath trees and recite poetry. I told her about Morecambe and Wise.

'Well, there was a tall, balding one who used to move his glasses to the side of his face and tease the other one, who had short, fat, hairy legs, and say he couldn't see the join in his hairline ...'

'He wore a wig?'

'No, it was all his own hair. Anyway, then he would slap him around the face ...'

'What? He would hit him?'

'No, no. They were best friends. They used to live together. Some of the sketches they did were set in their double bed.'

'...?'

After a while I gave up trying to explain to her. Maybe you had to be there.

*Ernie is sitting up in bed scribbling some notes on a piece of
paper. Another masterpiece. Eric walks in to the room, takes
off his dressing gown and gets into bed with Ernie. He lights
his pipe. Bored. Eric starts talking but Ernie doesn't want to
be diverted. Eric sits there making a succession of stupid
comments, but Ernie won't be distracted.*

*Eric complains that it's cold on his side of the bed. Will Ernie
swap sides? No. Eric's still bored. He gets out of bed and goes
over to the window. Nothing much is happening. We hear the
siren of, maybe, a police car going by. Eric turns round, takes
the pipe out of his mouth.*

'He's not going to sell much ice-cream going at that speed.'

FOREWORD
by Joan Morecambe

It is said that you get over it in time. Well, you don't, but you do learn to accept it. It is thirteen years since Eric died, so why does it seem like last year?

WHAT HAS BEEN AN ENORMOUS consolation is the way in which the Morecambe and Wise shows are still in demand, and a new audience of young people are growing up and enjoying their humour. How thrilled Eric would be, and how satisfying it must be for Ernie in his retirement.

Given that several books on the lives of Morecambe and Wise have already been published, and a play about Eric's life, written by my son Gary, has been produced, it is a still greater tribute that Jeremy Novick decided to write this.

Memories of the early days remain vivid. Meeting Eric and Ernie for the first time at the Empire Theatre, Edinburgh; watching them from the wings and thinking they were terrific. I had not the slightest doubt that they would ultimately become stars; Eric pursuing me all week! His certainty that he would marry me. Of course he did, and we stayed happily married for 32 years.

What full, busy, sometimes frantic and varied years they were - due, naturally to the rise and rise of Morecambe and Wise. From the tough days of touring variety theatres week after week, interspersed with long runs of pantomime and summer seasons, to the early days of television - also tough in its own different way.

The years of blossoming into great stars in TV, and enjoying that elusive gift, the love of the nation. It is something given to few.

The Royal Command shows; their appearance one Christmas at Windsor Castle for the Queen; the TV shows in the USA, and appearing in theatres in Australia and Canada. The list goes on. Moments of great pride, such as receiving their OBE's at Buckingham Palace, followed by the Freedom of the City of London.

Eric's enormous pride in receiving an honorary degree from Lancaster University. He was also very proud of becoming President for that great charitable organisation, The Lord's Taverners', and worked so hard for them over a three year period. Little could he have dreamed that from the Lord Taverners', a new arm, the Lady Taverners', would be formed, and that I would become their founding president.

What of the future? Ernie and Doreen are enjoying their retirement, and in spite of the problems with Ernie's health, they manage to travel a lot and spend time enjoying the sunshine in Florida.

As for the Morecambe clan, the two grandchildren Eric so loved as tots are now young people he would be proud of, full of life, and bitten by the showbiz bug. I guess it had to come out.

Gary and his wife Tracey, presented me with a further four grandchildren. The great sadness is that they will never know their grandfather, and he will never know them. Although perhaps one of the three boys will follow in Eric's footsteps.

Sitting in a row one night, watching one of the many and often Morecambe and Wise television repeats, and looking unsure of what it was all about, Gary asked his sons, "Do you like the show?"

One replied surely and instantly. "Well, I like the one with the glasses!"

THAT WAS THEN

IN TERMS OF THE DEVELOPMENT of Britain's television age, Morecambe and Wise – or rather, *The Morecambe And Wise Show* – appeared at exactly the right time. As the 1960s turned into the 70s, we were one nation united by a television screen. This was the era of three channel television. Cables were still attached to wirelesses, satellites only existed in James Bond films and Rupert Murdoch was selling advertising space on the Darwin Gazette ...

We were on the cusp between what was and what was to come. Television had just moved away from being if not an elitist tool, then not far from that. It was accessible to all, cheap enough to be truly a mass medium. It was no longer a mystery. Nearly every household had one, and the days had long gone when people would gaze in wonder at the white spot disappearing at the end of the day. Yet it wasn't so cheap that families had more than one set. There was no little Johnny disappearing up to his room to watch *Alien Death Zone* on Sky's new Zombie TV channel. If little Johnny wanted to watch television, he watched whatever his parents were watching.

How many of us grew up sitting around the television as a family watching Morecambe and Wise, getting to know them, getting to know their jokes ... all as a family. They captured and united a cross-generational audience in a way that simply would not be possible now. Looking back, it was a gentler time, a time when things were a little less frenetic, a little less rushed. (Probably all dewy-eyed nostalgic nonsense, but that's the way it seems so that's the way it was.)

This was the world Morecambe and Wise emerged into. The world they finally left was a very different beast. The number of TV stations might have been the same but that was about it. Everyone had television sets – sets, not set. You could buy those little things that sat ever so nicely on top of the fridge – Sony Trinitrons. By the time that happened, Eric and Ernie were there. Legends.

Analysing comedy is a waste of time. It kills it. Let's not bother. But something like Morecambe and Wise was more than comedy – it was a phenomenon, the like of which we'll never see again. Everything about it conspired to make it special. When it was, how it was, who it was. Each of these things on its own would have secured its popularity, but together they created a national experience, an institution.

It's no coincidence that Eric and Ernie produced their best television work in front of a curtain. Mostly, they just stood there talking as if to a real audience, not to some huge mythic outpost in Tellyland. For many viewers it was a real throwback to the good old days of the live theatre, the music hall they still remembered. In short, Morecambe and Wise hit their peak at exactly the right time. Five years earlier and they might have been left behind. Five years later and they might have been just another Two Ronnies.

Says Angela Rippon, who appeared on their show in 1976: 'I think a lot of comedians, sadly, nowadays delight in belittling people with their humour which Eric and Ernie never did. They had this wonderful wholesome reputation and they wrapped themselves and that reputation around the person they were dealing with so you were seen in the same light as them. The great skill they had was to be funny without being cruel and I think that's why everyone who appeared with them felt comfortable – because there was never any cruelty, there was never an attitude of "We're going to make you look a complete prat so that we look really good." That never ever came into the equation.'

They were consummately professional. Despite everything we knew, it looked for all the world like they weren't trying, that they'd just stumbled on to the stage. But that's how it is when you do your job well. Less accomplished entertainers try too hard to make you like them. Eric and Ernie never bothered with that nonsense.

They brought to television comedy a set of skills gained during their years on the stage, skills the generations that followed could never have. Like the ability to slip effortlessly into a soft-shoe shuffle, to know how to wear a top hat and tails. They had a sense of timing you can't buy. When to speak quickly, slowly, when to be loud or soft – they instinctively knew.

They came from an era of – and this is meant in the truest sense – gentlemen. They never swore. They weren't dirty. They weren't political. They didn't get cheap laughs by picking on the weak, making fun of those with speech impediments or physical disabilities. They'd spent years – *years* – getting to where they were and it made them humble. They liked their audience and they wanted to please them.

We could go on and on, but you get the point. There's an interesting game we could play here. Take all those points and apply them to comics that have come along since. Can you think of one who'd pass the Morecambe and Wise test? (Save your time. I've tried.)

Ultimately, it comes back to one thing – their training. Where they came from. It's depressing saying this because it makes me sound like my parents but really, it is all down to experience. By the time Morecambe and Wise hit the big time in 1970, they'd been at it for more than thirty years, playing off each other and learning each other's every tic.

It is interesting to contrast the duo with the generation of so-called alternative comedians that have come in their wake, especially the double acts like French and Saunders or Rik Mayall and Adrian Edmondson. None of them could wait to get into television. It's not something you can blame them for – after all, if someone comes to you and says, 'How would you like instant fame and fortune?', what are you going to do? Yet professionally, it's not done them or their audience any favours. The rapport that Morecambe and Wise had can only come with time – and that's the one thing TV doesn't allow. It's too competitive.

When they first got together, Eric was 12 and-a-half, Ernie was 13, two bright young things ready to take on the world. If that happened now they'd have a series on Channel 4 within, what, six months? But that's not how things worked in those days.

As TV mogul and former comedy producer Marcus Plantin said, 'You can't be a successful comic until you are in your late thirties. You need that sort of maturity. A lot of today's artists want to develop their careers in different ways. Morecambe and Wise didn't want to be writers, actors or producers. They stuck to what they did best which was their act.'

This isn't meant as some anti-youth sentiment – if you're good enough, you're old enough – but it's interesting to note that all the critics and commentators and all his contemporaries thought Eddie Izzard was mad when he refused to appear on television. He still refused. And who's one of the most sought-after comics now?

Izzard was right. Not only does television eat your material, it robs you of space to grow. You can't develop into yourself. And if you get it wrong, if you screw up, you'll soon see the other side of television. It's a very unforgiving medium.

People forget – or don't know – that Morecambe and Wise had their first television series in the mid-1950s and thought they were going to take

They never swore.
They weren't
dirty. They
weren't political.

They didn't get
cheap laughs
by picking on
the weak.

The subtlety would come later...

For a couple of young lads on the make it must have been a top way to spend your life.

Compare Eric to Vic Reeves and Chris Evans. The debt is obvious

over the world. After one show they were begging the producer to let them out of their contract. After four shows they tried to buy themselves out. The reviews – 'What's the definition of a television set? A box in which to bury Morecambe and Wise' – were killing. They weren't allowed the out, and it took seven years to get another shot, six spent in self-exposed exile, Eric in a sulk, disillusioned.

Maybe the years of struggle and toil and the northern clubs made Eric and Ernie appreciate what they had more. It's another horribly parental-sounding value, but maybe it's actually true. The harder you work for something, the more you appreciate it.

It's been said that Morecambe and Wise haven't dated, and that the reason for this is that there's nothing resembling satire in their shows. Neither of these statements is true. Their shows are inevitably time-locked – by the references, the guests, the size of the shirt collars. Satire has very little to do with it.

What is curious, though, is that their shows demonstrate that much more has changed in the past ten years than changed in the previous forty. Many of the routines Eric and Ernie made famous could have come from any point in their career. Assuming it's up to it, you could take a sketch from one of their early-60s shows, put it in a pair of flares, give it an elephantine shirt collar and place it in the mid-70s.

Compare Eric Morecambe to some of today's comics – notably Vic Reeves and Chris Evans. The debt is obvious. Evans used to end his shows by playing Bring Me Sunshine. Reeves? It's said his wife threatened to divorce him if he didn't stop playing Morecambe and Wise videos. But today's models have very little of Eric's generosity of spirit. There's an underlying aggression that just didn't exist back then.

The world was changing, and you can see it through Eric and Ernie. Similar models of humour today are full of verbal violence and aggression and rely heavily on shock tactics. Morecambe and Wise used none of those things. They cut across all ages, all classes.

They never offended and they had no social or political axe to grind. And that's what dates them.

LADIES AND GENTLEMEN, CARSON AND KID!

'It was fate. I pulled the Christmas cracker and he was in it.'

ERIC MORECAMBE

ON 27 NOVEMBER 1925, Ernest Wiseman was born to Harry and Connie in a small town called East Ardsley, somewhere between Wakefield and Leeds. It's a world where football means Rugby League football. Big men in big stripy shirts running into each other – hard – and there's no fancy Dan Bosman nonsense with your foreign imports and your garlicky ways. It was a world where peas were strictly mushy.

Harry was a good man. A bit of a spendthrift, a bit of a dreamer, a bit of a 'nice bloke who's never going to amount to much'. Curiously, he had lied about his age to get *into* the army for the first world war (he was that kind of man) and had won the Military Medal for saving his sergeant's life. Now he was a railway porter making £2 a week which wasn't much, even in East Ardsley in 1925.

Connie was born into a family three notches higher than Harry's on the Posh-O-Meter. Her father was dour, but that was nothing to make a note of. He was a Yorkshireman and it was in the contract. The Military Medal nonsense cut no ice with him and he told Connie, in no uncertain terms, that he disapproved. If she married Harry, he'd cut her off. (It's a tangential point, but sometimes people are so stupid. Irate fathers have probably been saying much the same thing since the dawn of time. 'He's no good for you.' Really? What do they think the daughter's going to do exactly?) So Connie married him and found herself cut off.

They were poor but happy in a way that now doesn't seem real. A house by the railway line that rumbled every time a train went by. An outside loo. A big galvanised iron bath that was dragged in and filled with hot water from the big iron kettle. Bread and dripping for tea.

What made the Wiseman family different was that they were a bit musical. When her father cast her out, the only things Connie took were her body and her piano which she played, according to Ernie, 'beautifully'. Harry was a performer, supplementing his paltry porter's wages by doing turns in the local working men's clubs. Beer and sandwiches and shirts with rigid collars which came off. And that's where it all started.

Ernie, the eldest of the five kids, wanted to please his dad. After being taken to watch him perform one day, Ernie decided the best way to please Dad would be to entertain. So he persuaded his mum to teach him a tune (The Sheikh Of Araby) and then he waited for his dad to come home. A few tap dancing lessons later and … 'Now give order for the next act on the bill which is going to be, ladies and gentlemen, Carson And Kid!'

Slip your mind into black and white for a moment. Television was in the future. Sonic was a frequency, not a hedgehog in a blue rinse, and as for the idea of an Italian superhero plumber called Mario … It was in this setting that Harry Wiseman took his eight-year-old son into his act

Eric was cool – honest

and onto the stage. Ernie was the 'cheeky little chappie. I'd come on and do a clog dance and members of the audience used to throw pennies. We had no transport so we had to make sure we caught the last bus home. I remember my father pushing through the queue to get on the bus.

There were seven of us at home, so we needed the extra money. On a good weekend, doing three shows, we'd earn as much as £3,10s.' Still, they never had any money. 'Father cut our hair,' remembers Ernie. 'We looked like a row of coconuts.'

MRS BARTHOLOMEW, YOUR BOY HAS TALENT – MAYBE WE CAN USE HIM

'Why did I want to become a comedian? Do you know, I don't know the answer to that. Or let me put it another way. I do know the answer. I never wanted to become a comedian. It was my mother who insisted on it and as she had a pretty strong personality, who was I to argue? She worked as an usherette at the end of Morecambe Pier and I suppose watching all those acts on the stage must have given her the idea that her little Eric could do just as well. And when my mother, God bless her, got a bee in her bonnet about something, there was no stopping her. I remember, she used to come home clutching a pile of programmes people had dropped or left behind, which she'd iron out in the kitchen until they looked like new. The next day she'd take them back to the theatre with her, sell them and bring home the money. Which wasn't for herself, you understand – it was money she'd invest in singing lessons for me. That's how determined she was to get me on the stage. Somehow that little lady saw something in me that she felt was worth nurturing and she devoted the rest of her life to doing just that. And, you know, the really amazing thing is that she spotted the same something in Ernie Wise.'

ERIC MORECAMBE

IT WAS MAY 1939, and John Eric Bartholomew had just received official notification that he'd won a local talent contest. Held at the northern seaside resort of Hoylake near Liverpool, the competition was typical of the many he'd entered. Don't put your daughter on the stage, Mrs Worthington? No one had ever said that to Sadie, Eric's mum – or, at least, they hadn't said it to her face.

This competition was different, though, to most of the talentfests that Eric went in for. What made it different was the prize. It wasn't a cup or a trophy or anything you could touch; it was the future – a chance to audition for Jack Hylton, a big-league local impresario.

Hylton was touring a discoveries show around the north of England's music-hall circuit. He'd find new talent and then tout it around. It was a routine that needed to be updated constantly. New talent, fresh talent – Hylton ate it. For the talent, it was a chance to move into a different league, to prove yourself.

And so it was that Eric turned up with Sadie and set about his business. If ever there was a power behind the throne, it was Sadie. Seeing Eric onto the audition stage, she said to him, 'Now go out there and give them all you've got. Make the words clear. If you pull it off I'll buy you an airgun.'

Eric had a repertoire of about six things, including a comedy number called I'm Not All There; an impression of Bud Flanagan singing Underneath The Arches; a top-hat-and-tails Fred Astaire impression; and finally, an impression of G.H. Elliott, the 'chocolate-coloured coon'. Eric was 13, just.

'Mrs Bartholomew,' said Jack Hylton, 'your boy has talent – maybe we can use him.' Sitting next to Hylton was another young lad, a song-and-dance prodigy who'd tapped his way to adolescent fame. His name was Ernie Wise.

He, too, had taken the talent-contest route but, armed with the experience gained with his dad in the Carson And Kid shows, young Ernie had cleaned up. Fame had come his way after he'd appeared in an annual charity event in Bradford, which was a big deal in Yorkshire, called the Nignog Revue. I'll just repeat that for you. It was called the Nignog Revue.

Singing and dancing and tapping for all his worth, Ernie didn't know Jack Hylton was sitting in the audience, out to do a bit of shopping. In the blink of a fairytale eye, Ernie found himself at the Prince's Theatre in London appearing in a show called *Band Waggon*, headlined by Arthur Askey. The next day the papers were his.

'Fame In a Night For 13-Year-Old Comedian' and 'Railway Porter's Son A Star Overnight' were just two of the headlines that caught the eye. One review said, 'His timing and confidence are remarkable. At 13, he is an old-time performer.' From that moment on, Wise was Hylton's. He joined his company on a permanent basis. He joined his family. He went to live in his house.

'Mrs Bartholomew,' said Jack Hylton, 'your boy has talent. Maybe we can use him.' Curiously enough, Sadie Bartholomew was thinking exactly the same thing about Jack Hylton's boy.

Eric with a half-pint. And Ernie

IF IT COMES DOWN ON ITS EDGE, WE'LL GO TO WORK

'I became very fond of Ernie. He was such a nice, gentle boy. He was every bit as much to me as my own son. I treated them alike. If I knitted a pair of socks for one, I knitted a pair for the other. During the war, when things were short, if I got hold of something like an orange I kept it until I had two so they could have one each – together.'

SADIE BARTHOLOMEW

BORN IN THE TOWN OF ERIC … No. That's an old nonsense gag Eric would trot out when people said he named himself after his home town. Born in the town of Morecambe on the north-Lancashire coast, the Bartholomews, like the Wisemans, could be filed under 'Poor But Happy'. Salt of the earth. George was a labourer with the Morecambe Corporation, earning about 38s a week. Easy-going and cheerful, he loved life and was content with things just the way they were.

Sadie was a different proposition. A matriarch. A powerhouse. It wasn't that Sadie was ambitious for the things that we normally associate with ambition, it was just she knew what the story was. No one messed when Sadie was around. Sadie had her eye on Ernie and from that moment it was going to take something bigger and more determined than she was to stop her.

Eventually, the war finished and the theatres re-opened. Slowly, life dusted itself off and got back to business. Sadie sent Eric off around the country, doing his funny little I'm Not All There act in his cut-off dinner suit and his big glasses. One night, he was booked to play the Swansea

Empire. And so was Jack Hylton with his discoveries show, *Youth Takes A Bow*. Sadie moved.

She told Dennis Holman for *Eric & Ernie*, 'I became very fond of Ernie. He was such a nice, gentle boy. He was every bit as much to me as my own son. I treated them alike. If I knitted a pair of socks for one, I knitted a pair for the other. During the war, when things were short, if I got hold of something like an orange I kept it until I had two so they could have one each – together.'

The deal was cemented when they were playing a theatre in Coventry. The show reached the city a week after the Blitz and the boys – well, Sadie – decided it would be best to stay in Birmingham and commute. 'Have you ever tried travelling with two 15-year-old boys in a compartment in the blackout with both of them supercharged with adrenaline after a show? You couldn't talk sense to either of them, they would just spend the time bantering and exchanging gags. In sheer desperation, one night I said, 'Now look. Instead of all this malarkey, why don't you put your brains to some use? Try and do a double act of your own. All you need are a few fresh jokes and a song.'

Imagine, for a minute, a stage. Ernie Wise is standing there, waiting. On walks Eric. He's holding a fishing rod with an apple dangling from it.

Ernie: 'What are you doing?'

Eric: 'Fishing.'

Ernie: 'You need a worm to do that, not an apple.'

Eric (looking hurt): 'I know that. The worm's inside the apple.'

You couldn't date that sketch. It could have come from any of the Morecambe and Wise shows. But it didn't. It was both more humble and more pivotal than that. It was the first sketch Eric and Ernie ever did together. For the record, it wasn't the first gag they ever did together. That honour fell to this unpromising item – nicked, incidentally, from the repertoire of another act that used to tread the boards, a little-known double act called Carson And Kid.

Ernie: 'What shall we do today?'

Eric: 'Let's toss a coin. Heads we'll go to the dog-racing. Tails we'll go to the football. If it comes down on its edge, we'll go to work.'

THE SPICE OF LIFE

'You'll hear old pros tell you that the 20s were the heyday of music hall and that by 1939 it was already dying, that the cinema was killing it. Yet when we started, in 1939, variety was still doing good business. Indeed, it was booming.'

ERNIE WISE

STILL, LISTENING NOW to those stories of the old variety theatres is like hearing tales about Victorian England. Stories about the booker, a woman called Cissy Williams, or about the Glasgow Empire – the Graveyard of English Comics as it was known – conjure up a mental image of horse-drawn carriages, cobbled streets, dark, foggy evenings. It's strange to think we're talking about only forty years ago.

The acts, though, the acts. And the gags. Cyclists like the Wonder Wheelers, balancing acts such as Jacky, the Dutch boy who would balance on his hands on wooden blocks building up a pile of bricks … The tableau acts (men and women dressed in white riding white horses with white dogs). Axe-throwers, knife-throwers, rag-doll dancers, Egyptian hieroglyphic dancers, sand dancers, mechanical dancers. Speciality acts like Old Mother Riley and Kitty, illusionists like Lionel King. And, of course, Wilson, Keppel and Betty. Tattersall, who did a speciality 'vent' act with life-sized clockwork dummies which he built himself. Occasionally they would find themselves booked as the light relief on a nude roadshow. It was work.

It's a culture that is long gone. Gone, but replaced by what? The cinema? Television? The post-war policy of only paying huge sums to top-ranking American acts? It doesn't really matter. It's what cultures are for. If they didn't come and go – well, that would be the sign of a dead society, wouldn't it?

For a couple of young lads on the make,

though, it must have been a top way to spend your life. A bit of larking about, earning and learning. A nod and a wink to one of the dancing girls in the show. Maybe a cup of tea at the Lyons or the nearest Kardomah. As Harry Worth has said: 'Showbusiness is OK if it wasn't for that bit of unpleasantness between 6.15 and 10.45.'

Ernie was the comic and Eric the Wellma Boy – the one who comes on and enquires, 'Well, my boy …' only to be insulted. 'Even as the straight man, Eric got the big laughs,' Ernie said later.

Ernie tells of a prank that summed up the era. 'We got hold of a life-sized ventriloquist's dummy and put it in the loo backstage at the Central Pier in Blackpool. There was only one loo backstage for everybody. We pulled down the dummy's trousers, sat him down, left him and waited. For the next hour or so, we watched several girls come and go. They'd knock on the door, get no reply and push the door open. Then they'd see him. Of course, they'd be too embarrassed to look properly and see that it was a dummy. There was one girl who was really bursting to go and tried a few times in quick succession. After about her third attempt, we heard her saying to the others that she thought the person in the toilet was really just somebody's idea of a joke. Quickly, we whipped the dummy out and Eric went in and waited. The girl with the anxious bladder tried again. Only that time she found Eric!'

It was like life on a university campus where every student is an extrovert show-off. People

On the show Double Six with Eileen Dyson in 1957

living on top of each other (that sounds like the start of a Max Miller gag) and working together. Having a bit of a cavort. Every night you'd do your act then the next morning you'd rush out to see if the local paper had a review in it. It was a little ritual that everyone followed, but no one admitted to. As they revealed in *Eric & Ernie*.

Eric: 'It was a pleasant and easy life. We knew comics, steady old troupers, who made between £60 and £100 a week as second on the bill, who'd been doing a total of maybe twenty minutes a show for fifty-two weeks a year, using material not a word of which had been changed in the past two or three decades.'

That last line is a giveaway. The audiences, though healthy – the infamous Glasgow Empire held three thousand people and was rarely, if ever, less than full – were geographically spread

out. What were the chances of you seeing Morecambe and Wise in Liverpool and then again in London? It wasn't going to happen. There was no television or national newspaper coverage. So there was nothing to encourage anyone to change their act. After all, most of the audiences were seeing it for the first time. What difference did it make if you'd been doing it for twenty years?

The difference was this. You can give someone a plate of horse meat and tell them it's the best fillet steak and if they don't know any better, they'll believe you. The problem for British acts came when someone brought in a plate of best fillet steak. Suddenly horse didn't taste so good.

When the American comics came over with their swanky suits and the new jokes – new jokes! – well, suddenly the land was flushed with insurance salesmen. It killed off a lot of British comics overnight.

For Morecambe and Wise, though, the dawn of the American age was an eye-opener. More than that, it was a door opener. Not because they were any more enlightened or, really, any better than anyone else. But because first of all, they were still young. What were they? 25? 26? Still babies. They were ready, willing and able to learn. They weren't set in their ways. They were still developing their act, honing and refining. Second, they weren't a speciality comedy act. They didn't have funny costumes or masks. It was just them, there. All they needed to adjust was their material. And third, they weren't yet particularly successful, so they were still malleable.

Some of their material, though … Take the beard routine, which they nicked from Abbott and Costello. Ernie would start singing and dancing. Eric would appear. Ernie would tell him to get off and let him finish his song. Eric would then reappear the same as before, but with a cigar with a beard attached to it (when he took the cigar out of his mouth, the beard would come away). Anyway, Eric would go, then reappear with his back to Ernie. Ernie would shout at him to get off, Eric would turn round, Ernie would see the beard and apologise.

Eric: 'Oh, that's all right.'

Ernie: 'I know a fellow exactly like you.'

Eric: 'Tall, slim, distinguished-looking, wearing glasses?'

Ernie: 'Except you have a beard.'

And on it would go. The gag, of course, was that every so often Eric would take the beard off and mug it up to the audience.

It was a rubbish routine. It had been rubbish when Abbott and Costello had done it and it was rubbish when Morecambe and Wise did it. But it was a solid enough slapstick routine which sold a few minutes. And it was part of the learning process, part of the way forward.

Compare them with someone like Max Miller

with his funny check suits, plus-fours, comedy hat and blue material. He may have been a headliner while they were still hanging around the hem of the showbiz curtain, but he had no legs. His gags were leagues better, but he couldn't survive. He was too of the time.

A typical Max Miller was the story of the tightrope-walker who was doing his act over a gorge with a raging river below. To his surprise, who should he see coming towards him on the rope but a very attractive stunt girl.

'What should he do?' Miller asked the audience. 'Go back the way he came or toss himself off?'

When the Americans came over, they looked smart and sharp – no funny suits. And they told not so much gags as stories with gags in them. For a couple of young comics who were still on the learning curve, this time was the perfect place to be.

Eric crosses over on TV – the Piccadilly Palace Show

THE LAND OF THE WHELKS AND BELCH

THE LEARNING CURVE wasn't confined to the stage. As with students on a university campus, study sometimes came second to a preoccupation that was increasingly rearing it's head. As Eric put it: 'When we had the time to chase girls we didn't have the money and when we had the money we were working so hard we never had the time.'

Ernie had been courting Doreen for seven years when, in the spring of 1952, he was tackled about it. 'Now look here, young man. Are you or are you not going to make an honest woman of her?' It was one of those – the sort of chat you'd expect from a girl's dad after seven years of hanging around. Except it wasn't from Doreen's dad. It was from Eric's mum, Sadie. What chance did Ernie have?

Eric met Joan in June 1952 when they were playing the Edinburgh Empire. 'I remember it was bandcall on a Monday morning. We used to look forward to bandcall to study form – there were always pretty girls in the chorus line. It was fun making smart-alec approaches,' said Eric. Consider for a moment the 27-year-old Eric Morecambe. Young and single and surrounded by young and single women. Think about 'it was fun making smart-alec approaches'. It brings a smile to your face, doesn't it? Anyway. 'Then I saw this tall girl, very beautiful with wonderful eyes and a sort of sweetness that makes your knees buckle and I knew immediately she was the one for me for life. Yes, it was as sudden as that. I asked her out for coffee and promptly set about working out a devious plan of campaign with only one thing on my mind.'

In much the same way as Eric and Ernie were thrown together by the intimate world of music

'I felt like a mother with an unmarriageable daughter that's miraculously swept off her hands by an unsuspecting sailor.'

ERNIE WISE

hall – the same faces going round the circuit, bumping into each other now and again like dodgems going round a track – so Eric and Joan were united and reunited. They met each other three times in quick succession. The boys found themselves playing in Margate where, as luck would have it, Joan's mum ran a pub. Then Joan found herself playing in Morecambe. Stuck for somewhere to stay?

Sometimes events conspire with fate in such a way it would be churlish to say no. By December they were married. The courtship dance that had taken Ernie seven years to perform took Eric barely seven months. Well, there's a surprise.

Ernie was best man. 'I felt like a mother with an unmarriageable daughter that's miraculously swept off her hands by an unsuspecting sailor.' With that done, Ernie was free to do what he had to do. Well, that's one way of looking at it. The other way is that Morecambe and Wise were the consummate double act. (Actually, maybe that accolade should be reserved for Mike and Bernie Winters. The honeymoon after Mike got married? There were three people on it.) Once Eric got married, Ernie had very little in the way of choice. On 18 January 1953 – five weeks later – Ernie married Doreen in her home town of Peterborough and travelled straight up to

The courtship dance that had taken Ernie seven years to perform, took Eric barely seven months.

Well, there's a surprise.

Sheffield where the boys were in a panto. 'Somebody reserved us a compartment on the train to Sheffield – it must have been Ernie's dad. My Ern was never that romantic,' said Doreen. (It's funny how the more you find out about the world of showbiz, the more you realise it really is one non-stop round of glamour-puss parties and glitzy premieres.)

The following summer, 1953, Eric and Ernie hit Blackpool. For the performer on the make, Blackpool was the place to be. Remember, we're back in the days before cheap flights and charter holidays. Majorca hadn't even been built and the Costa Del Sol was still full of sunny Spaniards who had no idea what the good Lord had up his sleeve.

Blackpool was kicking. If you wanted glitz, Blackpool was the place to be. If you wanted glamour … Even the football club was on a high, with Sir Stanley Matthews holding court.

For punters it was a holiday Mecca; for performers it was a bank paying-in book. Neither side of the equation could lose. If you went down well in Blackpool in front of the 'whelks and belch' audience, that was it. You were made. And for Eric and Ernie, it was like taking candy from a baby. Even the normally cautious Ernie let it all go to his head, and started taking both golf and flying lessons. The trappings of the successful.

Word spread. Audiences grew. Radio came knocking. They'd first gone on radio in 1942 on a programme called *Strike A New Note*, but they weren't even ugly ducklings then, let alone swans. By the early 50s, though, they were big names on the Blackpool circuit and commanded a degree of respect. After learning their trade on shows like *Workers' Playtime* and *Variety Fanfare*, they were auditioned by the BBC for a show called *Variety Bandbox*. It was really only the southern edition of *Variety Fanfare*, but still. It was another rung on the ladder.

With Acker Bilk in '62 – the shows were live then

YOU'RE ONLY YOUNG ONCE

Ronnie Waldman: 'You boys are natural TV material.'
Eric and Ernie: 'We believe you.'
When Ronnie Waldman said something like that, the visual motif would be that large finger coming down from the heavens they use to advertise the National Lottery. It could be you. 'You boys are natural TV material.'
Same thing, really.

SOON ENOUGH THEY GOT their own radio series, *You're Only Young Once*, or YOYO as the show became known. Under the umbrella of the BBC Light Entertainment department, they were produced by a man on the way up called Johnny Ammonds. Remember that name. You might come across it again.

The world was changing faster than a chorus line's outfits. What was true yesterday, well, who was to say if it'd be true tomorrow? The old rules were changing and the old ways of doing things were changing, too. Months and months of slogging around the circuit? You could get more exposure doing fifteen minutes on the radio. But there wasn't the intimacy or the immediacy – who was to know if they liked you or not? – and so comics and variety acts started to develop a different approach.

But was it good? And, more importantly, did it like you? Radio could taker a mid-league variety performer and, in less than an hour, turn them into a headlining act. With that level of power comes a degree of fear. If radio could take you that high, could it not also take you down? The name John Gilbert was lurking in more than one or two heads. If you're thinking 'John who?', the point will have been made. John Gilbert was the movie star who was killed off by the advent of the talkies. A huge star in the silent movies, he simply could not make the transition to the new era. Gilbert was a hunk, a real piece of meat. But

then they put a microphone under his nose and … this little squeaky voice popped out. Shortly after, he decided on a new career in a new bottle.

However, once they'd mastered the medium, Morecambe and Wise were away. A one-off spot on a TV programme opened the next door.

Ronnie Waldman: 'You boys are natural TV material.'

Eric and Ernie: 'We believe you.'

When Ronnie Waldman said something like that, the visual motif would be that large finger coming down from the heavens that they use to advertise the National Lottery. It could be you. 'You boys are natural TV material.' Same thing, really.

Eric and Ernie had been treading the boards since time began, but in the real world they were still only 28 years old. Young guns with a future to make. And so it was that on 21 April 1954, *Running Wild* burst forth from the television screens of a nation. Out of the screen and into our hearts. Out of the screen and into the Premiership. Out of the screen and on to the road to Hollywood.

'What'd the definition of a television? – a box in which to bury Morecambe and Wise.'

'How do two commonplace performers such as these get elevated to the position of having a series built around them?'

It was supposed to be a six-part series, but after the first show Eric and Ernie went to

Waldman and pleaded with him to be released from their contract. 'Not on your life,' said Ronnie. 'I'm going to hold you to that contract, not because I'm being bloody-minded or because I can't find anybody else to do me a half-hour comedy series every fortnight – most young comics would give their right arm for a chance like this. No, I'm doing it because I believe you are first-rate TV comedy material.'

If the reviews could have got any worse, they would have. But if you're a critic and you start off with, 'How dare they put such mediocre talent on television?', where do you go? Still Ronnie held firm. It could be you. Could it really?

Ernie: 'Eric was very upset, but one has to keep going, you know. Showbusiness. He'd get depressed about the criticism and I had to talk him out of it and cheer him up. I always used to boost his ego.'

Hollywood Schmollywood. The first engagement Morecambe and Wise got after their big TV break was fourth on the bill at the Ardwick Hippodrome in Manchester. Maybe it was God's way of keeping their feet on the ground. Or maybe it was something altogether more fundamental.

Eric told Ernie: 'We need a new act with new material. We've been too static. Not only that, but let's start putting our own personalities across.'

Hollywood Schmollywood. The first engagement Morecambe and Wise got

after their big TV break was fourth on the bill at the Ardwick Hippodrome, Manchester.

DAWN

'Hello, it's Billy Marsh.'
'Hello Billy. What's the story?'
'Leslie Grade has just been on the
phone about you two.'
'Oh yes. What did he say?'
'He said, "It could be you".'

WOUNDS HEAL. Sometimes they leave a scar, but more often than not, that's not a terrible thing. With a bit of luck, the scar is somewhere you can't see it. The scar Ernie got (that he's still got) from one of his stress boils is just below the shirt collar line. But sometimes you can't see the scars at all because they're not on the skin, they're on the soul. But still. Wounds heal.

By the following Christmas Eric and Ernie were billing themselves as 'those inimitable TV comedians'. Look, if you didn't have a thick skin you wouldn't be on that stage and Eric and Ernie had been on it for twenty years. Anyway, they weren't even 30 years old yet.

The next time opportunity came knocking, they were ready. Johnny Speight was lined up to write a few spots for Winifred Atwell's ITV series. And Speight knew what he was doing. Best let the boys' personalities come through, he reasoned. Don't be too structured. Don't suffocate them. That was the theory, anyway.

On 21 April 1956, they came to do the first show. Live. The opening sketch was a quick one-off gag. Eric's standing on the stage. He's drunk. A taxi comes by and he hails it. He gets in one door and goes straight out the other.

'How much, driver?' he says.

'Ten shillings,' Ernie replies.

'OK,' says Eric. 'But next time don't drive so fast.'

And off the cab goes. Gag done.

It's not a bad gag. It's not going to stop the world, but it's not a bad gag. Or at least it wouldn't have been a bad gag. But the gag didn't actually happen like that.

The taxi wasn't allowed to drive on and off the stage because of regulations on exhaust fumes in enclosed areas, so a reasonably simple rope-pulley system was rigged up. The taxi was pulled on and the taxi would be pulled off. But. When the gag ended and the taxi was due to drive off, as a reflex action Ernie put it into gear. He didn't think about it, he just put it into gear. And the car wouldn't move. Technicians went into a frenzy and tried to get the car offstage. But it wouldn't move. And this, remember, was live television.

Like someone relieved of a heavy overcoat and feeling freed, Eric started ad-libbing. Still in drunk mode, he was pushing the car, getting into the passenger seat offering advice to the hapless Ernie who got the hint and started ad-libbing back. Eventually someone realised what had happened and the car slid gracefully offstage. Eric and Ernie came off thinking that, well, that was that. Maybe television just wasn't for them.

The sketch made them. The producer, Dickie Leeman, liked their ad-lib response so much he made sure something went wrong the following week. And the week after that.

It says much for their state of mind at this time that Eric and Ernie decided to take an eight-month break from their relentless schedule. OK, so they knew they had a summer season in Blackpool booked and OK, it wasn't all holiday – they'd booked some dates in Australia – but it was eight months off and, more importantly, eight months away.

During that winter of 1958-9, a strange thing happened. Eric and Ernie (and Joan and Doreen) left the Old World and went to the New World but when they returned to the Old World, they found it wasn't there anymore. Gone. The world – their world – was a changed place. While Morecambe and Wise had been off gallivanting in foreign climes, there'd been a death in the family. Variety had died. Or, more accurately, it had been killed. It looked like murder, and television had its prints all over the murder weapon.

Still, figured Eric and Ernie, you can't worry

about what was. As their last experience of television had been a happy one, they weren't too concerned. In an act of rare callousness, they dumped their agent, Frank Pope, and set about getting a new one with good TV connections. No disrespect to Frank, it was just they had to move with the times.

Billy Marsh was the man with the plan. He was known to have a good relationship with Bernard Delfont and if you had a good relationship with Delfont then you had a good relationship with television.

'That's it,' said Billy after they'd shaken hands. 'But remember television is not like touring in variety. Television gobbles up material – you can't use it again. It means providing instant, personalised comedy. Your stage experience won't help very much except perhaps in your timing. It's a totally different medium that few stage people really appreciate. But if you can keep coming up with good, fresh stuff, I can get you all the television you want.'

And he did. By the end of the year, as the new decade dawned, they were everywhere. *Saturday Night At The Prince Of Wales, Val Parnell's Sunday Night At The London Palladium, Saturday Spectacular, Star Time…* If there was a big-bill variety show, they were on it. They were on everything except the one thing they really wanted to be on – their own show.

The phone rang the following June.

'Hello, it's Billy Marsh.'

'Hello Billy. What's the story?'

'Leslie Grade has just been on the phone about you two.'

'Oh yes. What did he say?'

'He said, "It could be you".'

A big show for ATV. Live. Thursday nights for a thirteen-week season. It was exactly what they wanted. And because it was exactly what they wanted, they had nerves like never before. The thing was this. They could do stand-up in a Palladium or an Empire till the cows came home. They could play an audience, hold it. That was OK. They could also do all the *Saturday Night At This Place*-type of shows they wanted and that was OK, too. What did you do

on those shows? Eight minutes if you were lucky – you were laughing. This deal was different. They weren't going to be guest-starring on someone else's show. They weren't going to be flying in and out. They were going to be the stars. And no one had to remind them of the words *Running Wild*.

The key to success, it was pointed out to them, was to have the right people around you. Get the best writers and the best producer and it's no grief. Surround yourselves with mediocre talent, and … The logic was undeniable.

Sid Green and Dick Hills had furnished Jewel and Warriss, a top double act of the day, with good material for a TV show. They'd also written successfully for Dave King, Harry Secombe, Bruce Forsyth, Sid James, Lance Percival, Roy Castle, Charlie Drake and Tony Newley. If anyone could do the business for Morecambe and Wise, Eric and Ernie figured, it would be Green and Hills.

It was then they pulled off their masterstroke. They told Billy Marsh they wanted Green and Hills. Marsh made a few calls and … no. the answer was no. Maybe it was lack of dosh. Maybe it was Leslie Grade not wanting to be dictated to. Either way, it was no. So Eric and Ernie bit the bullet. No Green and Hills, they said, no Morecambe and Wise. This was big. They were being offered a headlining series, their own show, £400 a week. And they were saying that unless they got exactly what they wanted, they wouldn't do it. This was 1961 and people just didn't do that kind of thing. Well, not unless they were American, anyway. Or, as it turned out, Morecambe and Wise.

They were playing a season in Torquay when they got the call that their choice had been approved. The next day, Sid and Dick arrived in Torquay with a copy of Johnny Mercer's record Two Of A Kind.

Now. Remember the drunk and the taxi driver sketch? How it only really worked after it had gone wrong, how triumph had emerged out of adversity? Well, the same thing happened with Sid and Dick. They came with a real track record, a proper pedigree, yet their writing technique was, at best, unorthodox. They'd turn up at rehearsals with a piece of paper on which was written 'Our Ideas For The Week'. And nothing else. Then the four of them – Sid and Dick and Eric and Ernie – would sit down and discuss Our Ideas For The Week. And that would be the show.

Unlike Eric and Ernie, Sid and Dick favoured sketches which had loads of people milling around busily and wrote them accordingly. Eric: 'I remember a sketch in the first show in which Ernie and I were supposed to be spies. I pointed out there were so many people in the sketch that I couldn't find Ernie, but I was overruled. The experts knew what was good for us. The following week, they came up with an even more populated sketch. The jokes were there. We had some very funny lines, but again we were sure it was wrong for us.'

Now comes the Fate bit. Equity went on strike. The actors were no longer acting. The heavily populated Sid and Dick sketches were suddenly not so heavily populated. What could the poor boys do? Get Sid and Dick to rewrite? No. It was, of course, a message from above. It was exactly what they needed. It meant they could keep Sid and Dick sweet and get the type of sketches they wanted. Lots of Morecambe, lots of Wise, not so much of anybody else.

On one of these early shows, the Beatles were guests.

Colin Clews, the producer/director said later: 'After they'd done their bit I quietly remarked to someone, "I know we're doing six of these shows, but we'd better put out the

Improvisation, that was the key

one with the Beatles early in case they don't last."

What's more, they overheard me.'

Improvisation. That was the key. Instead of getting different actors to play different parts in the plays Sid and Dick wrote, Eric and Ernie played all the parts themselves. In itself, it looked like a huge gag. What did the watching telly audience know of what Sid and Dick had originally intended? The strike lasted three months and by the end of it, Eric and Ernie had a successful format.

Eric: 'It was remarkable how well we all gelled. We gained confidence from them and they gained confidence from us. There were arguments, plenty of them, but from those came the ideas.'

Eric (walking on stage with a yo-yo): 'I'm hooked. I've got to have my yo-yo all the time.'

Ernie: 'I can cure you of that.'

Eric: 'You can't. I'm a hopeless case.'

Ernie (pulling out a pair of scissors): 'Easy.'

MORROW, CAMBE AND WISE

'He began by introducing us as Morrow, Cambe and Wise and then looked around for the invisible third man. On top of that he described us as a European act.'

ERIC MORECAMBE ON ED SULLIVAN

THERE'S SOMETHING ABOUT Morecambe and Wise that's so essentially British it seems absurd to think of them doing their act in America. There's no real reason why this should be so – after all, there have been plenty of American comics who've cleaned up over here. Why should it not happen the other way round? It's just that Eric, in particular, seems so, well, English – northern English, even – that the idea of him doing the act in front of Americans ... They're going to be puzzled, surely?

But thus it came to pass. In 1964 Eric and Ernie were doing a show at the London Palladium like they'd done a hundred times before. It's not meant to sound blasé – it's just that it was a regular show. The bill was regular – Eve Boswell, Pearl Carr, Teddy Johnston, Bruce Forsyth headlining – and the audience was regular. Except in the audience that night at the Palladium was Ed Sullivan – Mr American TV.

The Ed Sullivan Show was unlike anything in England at the time. It was a barometer for all that was good. If Mr Ed liked you, you were happy. If Mr Ed didn't like you ... well, had you considered another career? Once, in another not-too-distant time zone, the New York comic Jackie Mason had appeared on *The Ed Sullivan show*. Mason was Jewish, a former rabbi, and he was big and on the way to getting a whole lot bigger. But Sullivan said something to him on air and Mason answered him back and that was it. Sullivan scowled and Mason was dead. He reckoned it killed his career for

maybe twenty years. (It should be added that Mason's Jewishness didn't help endear him to Sullivan. Still, the story gives an example of Sullivan's power.)

Ed Sullivan liked Morecambe and Wise. He booked them for three slots on his show, a show which regularly pulled in over fifty million viewers.

Eric: 'Ed must have been 70. His show was nothing more than a simple stringing-together of a number of variety acts. He was undoubtedly the star yet he never appeared to actually do very much and most of what he did do he got wrong.' Mr Ed must have liked Eric and Ernie because after Eric corrected him –'We're British', not only did Ed spare their lives, he made a joke of it, playing Rule Britannia the next time they walked on to his show.

In fact, for some strange reason, Sullivan took a special liking to Eric and Ernie, inviting them out to dinner – unheard of for Mr Ed – and generally taking them under his wing. For their part, the boys acted like a couple of provincial Brits on the loose in the Big City – which was exactly what they were. They ordered ridiculous amounts of drink on room service and got drunk. Sid and Dick came over to join them. More drink. There's no business like showbusiness.

1963 and 64 were, for Eric Morecambe and Ernie Wise, the years the Lord did point his finger at them. Every time they opened the front door, there was the postman with yet another sack full of success. Getting Ed Sullivan to like the boys – he took them out to dinner! – might have seemed like God's little double-bluff gag, but it wasn't. The Great Agent In The Sky really was happy to sprinkle their path with copious amounts of gold dust. That's one way of looking at it. Or you could say that since almost before they could walk, Eric and Ernie had been working their kishkas off and now was payback time.

QUICKER, QUICKER, FASTER, FASTER

'Look, my mates at work will never believe me. Do me a favour. Before you go, could you sign this for me?' Before you go. Now Eric must have signed thousands of autographs, but never before had he remembered three words so vividly.

ANYONE WHO'S EVER BEEN self-employed will understand the attitude. It doesn't matter how well things are going or how in demand you seem to be, you're never so secure that you can say no to an offer of work. For entertainers, it must be twice as bad. They've got that insecurity, plus the ego that

needs feeding constantly. And if you're working a lot that means you're successful and if you're successful that means your ego is likely to be in overdrive. And if your ego's in overdrive and someone asks you to do something …

So when, in 1963, Rank asked Eric and Ernie to make a feature film, there wasn't a question of doubt. Despite a working schedule that Eric said saw him at his new Harpenden home a total of twenty days in its first year, they leapt at the chance to do a film. It was a step nearer the really big league. Again, it's one of the unwritten rules of success-seekers. The next rung up the ladder is always the really big league and, needless to say, the really big league is always the next rung up the ladder.

Written by Sid Green and Dick Hills, who had

From a show that worked to a film that stank – not such a smart move for The Intelligence Men

Eric and Ern get an early look at reviews of The Magnificent Two

also been the team behind the Norman Wisdom films, *The Intelligence Men* was a disaster with absolutely no mitigating factors. Checking through a few of the newspaper reviews of that time gives a flavour.

'An unspeakable British farce in which two stage and television comedians are fed through the Norman Wisdom sausage machine and come out looking as though they couldn't make a hyena laugh. What a shame, and what a waste for all concerned.' (*The Times*)

'Norman Wisdom, please come back.' (*Evening Standard*)

'*The Intelligence Men* reminded me of Abbott and Costello at their worst.' (*The Sun*)

'In *The Intelligence Men* we have to watch the ruination of two excellent comics in an embarrassingly unfunny skit.' (*Sunday Express*)

'A chaos of flat gags.' (*Observer*)

It's bad enough when a television sit-com is transferred to the big screen and made into a film. In recent years, it seems, the practice has finally stopped, but during the 1970s and 80s nearly every sit-com of note was given the big-screen treatment.

To say every attempt has been a complete disaster is not overstating the case.

Though it would be wrong to put all the blame on Hills and Green – they did, after all, write those seminal pre-1968 ATV shows – they made the classic mistake of changing the characters of Eric and Ernie, making Eric a bit of a simpleton, a bit of an idiot. The result was that the balance between the two was altered – fatal for a double act. Combine that with the inevitable loss of intimacy that a transfer to the big screen involves ...

There were, however, a couple of gags in *The Intelligence Men*. One was even smileworthy:

Ernie: 'The whole relationship between the east and the west depends on you.'

Eric: 'I'm not worried about that.'

Ernie: 'Why not?'

Eric: 'I'm from the north.'

It couldn't have been worse. Sadly, not even that's true. In the next two years they made *That Riviera Touch* and *The Magnificent Two*, films that made *The Intelligence Men* look like *The Godfather*. 'While we were making *The Magnificent Two* the James Bond film *You Only Live Twice* was being shot

at the same studios, Pinewood,' said Ernie in his autobiography. 'They built a volcano for £250,000, which was more than the entire budget for our film.'

There is another, far simpler, explanation for why their films didn't work. They were, as Eric was to say later and in a different context, 'ruggish'. They were awful. The scripts were awful. Eric and Ernie might have been great comics, great song-and-dance men (though whether Ernie was, as he claimed, in the Gene Kelly class ...), Eric and Ernie might have been any number of things. But actors? No. Ruggish.

Meanwhile, Joan was getting more and more worried about Eric. Ernie: 'He was smoking between sixty and a hundred cigarettes a day and living on his nerves. None of those who worked with him, including myself, quite appreciated the pressures he was under. Eric, on the surface, has a very bland manner and an even blander sense of humour. At the same time he's a hypochondriac with never any qualms about letting you know of every twinge he suffers.'

Like hamsters on a wheel, Eric and Ernie were running quicker and quicker, moving faster and faster, doing more and more, just to keep pace with their own success. In the mid-60s, they were going from strength to strength. As long as they stayed away from Pinewood Studios and its mendacious dreams of Hollywood and Vegas, they could do no wrong. A summer show at Great Yarmouth broke all records. A record of a different kind, An Evening With Ernie Wise At Eric Morecambe's Place, was a success. A thirteen-part colour television series had just been sold

to North America and had been very well received. (Well, it had been very well received in Canada, but that's North America too). Most importantly, in 1968 they moved from ITV to the BBC, lured by the promise of a colour show and much more money.

With the success came more success. Still they couldn't say no. Some of their decisions seem bizarre. An offer to star in a West End show, something which only a few years earlier they'd have given anything to do, was turned down in favour of going on a tour of the northern clubs. Why? Because the clubs paid better. The work ethic is admirable. The financial imperative undeniable. But a smart thing to do? For lots of reasons it would have made sense to take the West End option. They'd have got more attention which would, in the longer term, have produced better contracts. They'd have moved on to a different level – a swankier plane. More showbiz, less sweat. And they wouldn't have had to work so hard.

But it's easy to be wise after the event … it's not even a good pun. The point is, yet again, this was their heritage coming through. They came from that northern club background which said you worked. The working class weren't called the working class for nothing. It's what you did.

It's worth remembering here that Eric and Ernie were 42. It's really not very old. 'We'd gone twenty-seven years without ever missing a performance. We both knew the number-one threat in our business was your health. We'd been telling each other to take it easy.'

But still. Off they went to Yorkshire to the northern showbiz phenomenon that was the Batley Variety Club. The biggest and best of its kind, it attracted huge crowds and the very top acts. Opening a season there on Sunday, 3 November 1968, they did a ninety-minute gig which started at midnight.

By the Thursday, Eric wasn't feeling well. Pain in the chest. A twinge in the arm. A bit short of breath, off-balance. 'Ernie,' he said, 'if you don't mind I'll go straight back to my hotel.' He left Ernie to sign the autograph books that were brought to the dressing room after the show. Hypochondriac.

There's a story Eric told about how he was driving back to his hotel in his Jensen Interceptor when the pains told him to take a detour via the casualty unit. He was helped through to the X-ray department by a passer-by who'd recognised him and lent a hand. The man asked Eric for an autograph. 'Look, my mates at work will never believe me. Do me a favour. Before you go, could you sign this for me.' Before you go. Now Eric must have signed thousands of autographs, but never before had he remembered three words so vividly.

It was a major heart attack. Not fatal but major, and it forced a number of changes for both Morecambe and Wise as an act and Eric as a person. It took them out of the game for six months, forcing them to retire and Eric to take up a second career as a birdwatcher. As for Ernie, he did a little bit of this and that, kept his hand in. And everything he made, he split with Eric. 'It wasn't an easy position for me to be in. I couldn't very well go out and start doing things on my own – not that I wanted to – until something definite was settled about Eric's future. If a doctor had said he would never work again, that would have put a completely different complexion on it. In the meantime, I had to stand by him, as I am sure he would have done by me.'

Life has a curious way of taking decisions on your behalf that at the time feel like complete body blows and yet years later seem absolutely right. You lose your job and it's the end of the world, but it turns out your new job is better than the old one in every way. If you hadn't lost your job in the first place, you'd never have bothered looking for the other one. Different religions have different words for it, but for now let's just call it life.

During this six-month sabbatical, Sid and Dick were poached by ATV and signed an exclusive deal. Eric and Ernie were with the BBC, and that was that. Being temporarily out of the game, Eric and Ernie knew nothing about this. Ernie tells the story now: 'I was on a flight between New York and Barbados – can't be bad, eh – when one of the stewards came up to me and said, "What are you going to do now that your writers have gone?" I didn't know what he was talking about. I hadn't heard anything.' It's nice that even after all these years of fame and fortune, Ernie still thinks it a big deal to be on a flight from New York to Barbados.

The head of Light Entertainment at the BBC, Billy Cotton Jr (Billy 'Wakey, wakey' Cotton's son – and if that doesn't make you feel old, nothing will), had been exceptionally good and loyal. Not only did he honour their existing contract when no one even knew if

they'd work again, he also signed them up to another contract for thirteen shows a year for the next three years. And that's how they came into contact with Eddie Braben. Braben, 38 when he teamed up with Morecambe and Wise, had been Ken Dodd's gag writer for the previous twelve years. It seems a haphazard choice, but in fact it shows that Cotton knew exactly what he was doing.

Eddie Braben: 'Really I'm only a gag man. I've never done situations and sketches.'

Billy Cotton Jr: 'I'll tell you what. We'll suggest a few ideas and situations, and you can go away and write the boys a show. How's that sound?'

There were three feature films in three years – all of them 'ruggish'. Though there were, of course, some good things to be said for making movies

It was a major heart attack. Not fatal but major, and it forced a number of changes for both Morecambe and Wise, and Eric as a person.

Eric and Ern show Christine Pockett how to dance the Spanish way, on Piccadilly Palace.

Millicent Martin tries an Apache dance with Eric and Ern on Piccadilly Palace

Life has a curious way of taking decisions on your behalf that, at the time, feel like complete body blows and yet, years later, seem absolutely right.

BRING ME SUNSHINE

'All men are fools and what makes them so is having beauty like what I have got.'

GLENDA JACKSON AS CLEOPATRA

AS SOON AS MORECAMBE AND WISE started working with Braben, it was obvious he made the difference. Out came all the catchphrases and gags that have become part of the national vocabulary. You can't see the join. Short, fat, hairy legs. The stare into the camera. Pardon? Can he say that? And on and on. Ernie's character changed, became more closely defined. He was mean, egocentric, vain.

Whereas Hills and Green used to come in with their blank bit of paper but end up writing everything – every word, every nod, every wink – Braben just wrote the words. Eric and Ernie and, crucially, the producer Johnny Ammonds filled in the rest. Sweetly as Eddie fitted in, much of the credit must go to Ammonds. He'd first worked with them twenty years before on the much maligned *Vanity Fair* but since then had made a big name for himself as a producer of the Harry Worth and Val Doonican shows.

It's easy to see the connection between those two shows and Morecambe and Wise. If there's any memory of them, it is of the visual motifs both carried. Harry Worth standing on one side of a mirror and raising a leg and an arm so that in the reflection it looked like he was raising all four limbs. It sounds ridiculous now, but at the time it was very funny. This little man in his Harold Wilson mac and his trilby spread-eagled in mid-air.

Similarly the overriding memory of Val Doonican is of him wearing a nice pully, swaying in his rocking chair, singing.

It comes as no surprise, then, to learn that it was Ammonds who suggested the Bring Me Sunshine dance. A strong visual motif to lock the pair in the public eye.

Reading Eddie Braben's scripts now, you cannot help but smile. You can try, but it won't do any good. (At this juncture it's worth recalling what Barry Cryer said about his time as a scriptwriter for Frankie Howerd, that he had to write all the 'No, listen' and 'oohs' and 'aahhs' into the script. All Frankie's asides, those ad-libs that made him what he was, all those knowing nods, were written for him. It's worth recalling that if only to recognise Eddie Braben for the writer that he was. As inspired as Eric and Ernie were, so was Braben.)

Just as in the 60s the ATV shows had had their regular items (a favourite was Wise promising Morecambe a plum role in a costume drama, then Morecambe would come on in costume only to be told 'we've run out of time'), the Braben/BBC years were marked by regular gags, routines and catchphrases that we all know and love, like best friends. The gags remained as classy as ever.

Ernie (accusingly): 'You grew that moustache for a girl.'

Eric: 'No I didn't. She grows her own.'

But more than anything, more than even

Waaay-hey! Get out of that, then

maybe the catchphrases, it's the plays what Ernie wrote that stick in the memory, plays that invariably featured one of the major stars of the day.

This is an important difference between the ATV era and the later BBC shows. In the early days, the guests were people like Kenny Ball and his Jazzmen doing King Of The Swingers (again and again) which was very sweet but rather symptomatic of the time. The light entertainment schedules were littered with interchangeable shows and guests who were equally interchangeable – largely because they were the same people. *The Cliff Richard Show* with special guest Lulu would the following week be *The Lulu Show* with special guest Clodagh Rodgers which in turn would become *The Lulu Show* with special guest Cliff Richard. It was a small world.

In the 60s, *The Morecambe And Wise Show* fitted into that scenario perfectly. Kenny Ball. And they would always have some refugees from the local Greek taverna in fancy dress calling themselves something like Los Spanakopitos. It looked like a gag, only it was for real.

Now we had something rather more ambitious. Big stars. Names from the top drawer. It was a brilliant idea – theirs, incidentally – which suited both sides perfectly. Morecambe and Wise are so popular they can pull Glenda Jackson. Or, Glenda Jackson is so popular Morecambe and Wise want her on their show. Who is the more flattered?

Once the tradition had been set it was easy to persuade stars of the highest order to appear on the show. They even got Laurence Olivier to appear, though it should be said he was more than a little suspicious, finally agreeing to do it as long as he didn't have to actually do anything. So they filmed him sitting at home, putting on different accents to avoid Eric who kept phoning up to ask if he'd be on the show.

It's not hard to see the appeal. Eric and Ernie were already a much-loved institution. By associating with them, the stars humanised themselves, made themselves more lovable. What's more, their faces became instantly recognisable to millions of viewers. What do you suppose people best remember Glenda Jackson for? Winning Oscars? *Women In Love*? Quitting showbiz and standing for parliament? Or for appearing on Morecambe and Wise and uttering the legendary words, 'All men are fools and what makes them so is having beauty like what I have got'? By appearing in the show, Glenda Jackson raised her profile by about fourteen light years and reached a section of the population which had previously only heard of her. Now they had seen her.

As for Eric and Ernie, it was a thrill. Meeting a famous person, getting them on their show.

Eric: 'We treated [Glenda Jackson] with a certain amount of awe when we first met her. Fortunately she took the sketch just as seriously as we did. Before she went on, she asked, "Am I doing this right?" All I said was, "Just make it louder and faster." So she played it loud and fast. She was great.'

Ernie – and this is a typical comment – added: 'The film producer Mel Frank saw Glenda on the show and said, "Gee, that girl can do comedy". He immediately offered her the lead in *A Touch Of Class*, and her performance won her an Oscar. Really, we felt a little insulted after he called her. He didn't offer us anything.'

For her part, Glenda said that working with Morecambe and Wise was 'the highlight of my career'.

It was genuinely funny, seeing proper stars having to say words like what they were saying and enjoying it so much. Letting their hair down and playing. Playing – maybe that's the key word. And it was lovely to see Eric and Ernie not so much pricking as destroying the pomposity of these great stars, for mostly that was the deal. 'Serious' celebrities like Glenda Jackson, Andre Previn, Robin Day, would come on and their reputations would be completely disregarded.

'I'll just get my baton ... It's in Chicago.' **ANDRE PREVIN**

Angela Rippon: 'That was the whole point of what they did. What happened in my situation was absolutely no different to what they did with Glenda or Andre Previn or whoever. People have a particular impression of you because of the job you do and, frankly if you are going to read the news ... The news is a serious business – you don't muck about, you do it absolutely straight. But that doesn't mean that's your entire persona. That's where they were so clever, because they picked people who had a public persona that was firmly rooted in the job they did. They could see behind that and bring out, in a very gentle and funny and amusing but loving way, the other side to them.

'That is why the Previn thing is so funny, why the Shirley Bassey thing is so funny and why Glenda Jackson went on to make the first comedy film she'd ever made and got an Oscar for it. Robin Day, similarly, went from being the scourge of every politician in the land to sitting there with a crash helmet on with his bow-tie going round in circles and a custard pie in his face. But never as a result of that sketch did he lose any dignity in his professional life. It was just that particular spot in the show became accepted as a moment where the person could let their hair down in the spirit of Christmas and have a laugh, and entertain people without losing their dignity.

'This was what they kept saying to me: "We want you to look good. We want you to feel good and look good", and I'm sure they said that to everybody who worked with them.

'And at the end of it you came out looking wonderful.'

HELLO FOLKS AND WHAT ABOUT THE WORKERS?

Cleopatra: 'Don't you find the desert romantic?'
Octavian Caesar: 'It's all right now, but what's it like when the tide comes in?'

THE ANTONY AND CLEOPATRA sketch in the 1971 Christmas show, starring Glenda Jackson as Queen Cleopatra, was possibly the classic play what Ernie wrote. The scene opens in a richly furnished apartment in Cleopatra's palace. Glenda enters to the theme music from *Dr Finlay's Casebook*. She looks puzzled but continues.

Desdemona (her handmaiden): 'My queen.'
Cleopatra: 'Has my lover arrived yet?'
Desdemona: 'Which one?'
Cleopatra: 'What day is it?'
Desdemona: 'Friday.'
Cleopatra (looks at diary): 'Mark Antony. Two till ten.'
Desdemona: 'He loves you terribly.'
Cleopatra: 'I keep telling him that. All men are fools. They place themselves at my feet and I use them as stepping stones.'

It's a perfect start. There are two jokes, both of which are dreadful, but what makes it so special like what it is (sorry, it's catching) is the grace with which Glenda plays her role, spitting out each word with distaste, like some kid receiving a nasty medicine in a Carry On film. Also, there's the anticipation of Eric and Ernie's entrances. Even when Ernie arrives, it's just a taster for Eric – it's only when Morecambe arrives that the thing really kicks off.

Eric enters to the music from *Match Of The Day*. He is wearing wellington boots and a busby hat and is dressed as a gladiator.

Octavian Caesar (Eric): 'Evening, all. Sorry I'm late only I've been irrigating the desert ... which isn't easy on your own.'
Cleopatra: 'Is Caesar with you?'
Octavian Caesar: 'No, he couldn't come. He's got the hieroglyphics.'
Cleopatra: 'You must be hungry after such a long journey. Can I get you some food?'
Octavian Caesar: 'Thank you all the same, but I've just had a couple of sheep's eyes. They'll see me through the day.'
Mark Antony (Ernie): 'And what is your business here?'
Octavian Caesar: 'I have been sent from Julius and Caesar.'
Cleopatra: Julius and Caesar?'
Octavian Caesar: 'I'm afraid so. A slight accident whilst polishing his sword.'
Cleopatra: 'Am I right in assuming that you have been sent here with the sole object of spying on me?'
Octavian Caesar: 'Is there anything to spy on?'
Cleopatra: 'Meaning?'
Octavian Caesar: 'You and the little chap here. Have you been ... a touch of hello folks and what about the workers?'
Cleopatra: 'All men are fools, and what makes them so is having beauty like what I have got.'

And on and on. The torrent of gags never stops, never even slows.

Cleopatra: 'What do you think of the pyramids?'
Octavian Caesar: 'Excellent. Their last record was a belter.'
Cleopatra: 'Don't you find the desert romantic?'
Octavian Caesar: 'It's all right now, but what's it like when the tide comes in?'

Just close your eyes and picture him saying, 'It's all right now, but what's it like when the tide comes in?'

You simply cannot deny it.

Ern shows off his hieroglyphics, Eric looks for the join

IT'S SHOWTIME

'Basically I'm a ham and I love to bring that kind of gloss to the screen. They loved it because Ernie and Eric were Hollywood-mad. We all used to talk about the great Hollywood movies, the world of make-believe and with our limited budget we tried to do the same kind of thing, but always with laughs.'

ERNEST MAXIN

IN 1974 THEY DECIDED to take a break from television. As Eric said in the November: 'I feel we need a break. Ernie and I have been doing television continuously for seven years now. That's fourteen shows a year. With repeats, it's twenty-eight which is the same as one every fortnight.' Part of the problem was, Eric admitted, 'We are what we are – comedians, not actors. Ronnie Barker, for instance, has a tremendous advantage over us. He can be a comic and he can act in a series like *Porridge*. Ernie and I can't do that. Even in a film we can only play ourselves.'

If it was a break, it was a very Morecambe and Wise break – i.e., no break at all. The Great British Public wasn't going to do without the Christmas special – there are some traditions that couldn't be messed with: turkey, trees, Morecambe and Wise – and the BBC put out a 'Best Of' compilation presented by Michael Parkinson followed by a set of repeats from their last series. The boys, meanwhile, decided to use their break by doing what they did best. They went back to doing live shows, their 'bank raids' as they called them.

Shortly afterwards, Ernest Maxin replaced Johnny Ammonds as the producer of the show and things moved up a notch. Nothing against Ammonds – he'd done some marvellous stuff with Eric and Ernie and, you could argue, made them what they were – but it was time for a new dimension and Maxin was the man to provide that.

Maxin was from the same shop as Eric and Ernie. OK, so he was Jewish and from the East End of London, but that's detail. He was from the same honest, working-class background. In his late-teens, Maxin had been a boxer. Neither Eric nor Ernie would ever have done that. Maxin became a boxer because if you were Jewish and working-class and you were a performer you became a boxer. And that's what he was – a performer.

A song and dance man who'd been brought up in the theatre, showbusiness was in the family. His aunt ran a digs for travelling-theatre types, and tales of the boards reverberated around the Maxin dinner table. His father taught him to play the piano, stretching his fingers gently every night. Hungry for the tales and anecdotes that thrilled his young mind, Ernest hung around theatres and stage doors, dining on the atmosphere. Word soon got around and one day the leader of the touring *Black And White Minstrels Show* came knocking. He asked Ernest's dad if his little boy would like to come on tour with them. Dad was indignant. The Black and White Minstrels? It was jazz! No son of mine is ever going to play jazz.

Ernest's time with the Black and White Minstrels – you didn't really think that he'd listen to his dad? – was over before he was into his teens. A big lad, by the time he was 9 years old his feet reached the floor from the piano stool and that was that. The novelty of having a kid on stage was gone.

But Ernest was hooked. Show followed show. From front of stage, he went backstage as a director and producer. By the age of 22 he was producing musical shows for the BBC. It was in his blood. Like Eric and Ernie, he never really stood a chance.

'I was always Hollywood-mad – you know, film-mad. Gene Kelly was my idol, you see, and Fred Astaire and the Sinatras. It was this great era and I loved Hollywood and all that glamour. The BBC sent me on a technical course for six weeks and then gave me a show. My first show was with Petula Clark and I drove everybody mad by putting varnish all over the stage floor because I wanted everything to look glossy.'

Christmas 1972 – Oscar-winner Glenda Jackson comes back for more song and dance

Ernest Maxim had the boys dust down their old song-and-dance skills – 'I tried to bring a touch of Hollywood to it'

By 1975, Ernest Maxin and Morecambe and Wise were on a collision course, but the show was still very much John Ammonds'. The shows were getting more and more popular and as they did, they got bigger and bigger and the stars got bigger, too. But Ammonds wasn't a big production-numbers type. He did comedy shows.

Maxin: 'John and I were great friends, and I was producing a Dave Allen show at the time, and John said to me: "Would you like to do something for Eric and Ernie? Have you got any ideas for a musical number for the show?" And I said, "Yeah". Anyway, this was for the Shirley Bassey number and I worked out this routine and wrote it up. Actually, I had done it a few years before but it was late at night and it was a man, you wouldn't know him, called Ormond Douglas. He was a very handsome Australian baritone singer, and he came over and he had a great voice and we did this routine with him –

the whole idea of the shoes getting caught and someone coming on from the side and putting another boot on. So I thought of that and said to John that I thought it would work and it worked very well, as you know. Shirley loved doing it.

'Then I did another routine for John and, you know, I used to love doing it because it was another outlet for me while I was doing my other shows. I did the routine with Cliff Richard with the boys as sailors when they were dancing on the deck and getting their feet caught in it and it was great fun.

'Then Bill Cotton called me into his office one day and said, "Eric and Ernie would like you to take over the show, they want you to produce and direct the show."

'And I said, "Well I think the show's doing pretty well as it is under John Ammonds." You know, he was doing great shows with them, their ratings were up over seventeen million. I said:

Half close your eyes, and it could be Fred Astaire and Gene Kelly. Oh alright then

The inspiration for the song and dance numbers came from old MGM musicals, so there were a lot of staircases

"Is it wise to change in mid-stream?" Bill said: "Well, the boys think you'd bring another dimension." I said: "Well that's just a matter of opinion, isn't it?"

'Anyway, Bill said I shouldn't worry because he had Mike Yarwood which he said he knew John Ammonds wanted to do. Then he asked me again. Would I take over *The Morecambe And Wise Show*? And I said I'd love to, but only as long as John's happy. It was important that John was happy because our offices were next door to each other. So I went to John and he said he didn't want to do it any more. He said, "I've had a good stint at it and maybe it's time for a new broom." That was in 1974.'

Eric and Ernie might have changed their producer and *The Morecambe And Wise Show* might have upped its ambitions, but the song, essentially, remained the same. Prick the pomposity of the star. Basically, either they were roped in to do a song-and-dance number or they took part in one of Ernie's plays what he wrote.

Staircases were a recurring motif in these shows. It was the MGM number in all three of them. In the early 60s, the great American comic Jack Benny had come over to do a show. Being a true professional, Benny had studied the form and said he'd only do a show in England if Ernest Maxin produced it. 'I made it like a big MGM musical. Those huge productions, those big sets, I loved it all.'

When his time came – when the money came – he let go. Out came the dinner suits, the top hats and tails, the sticks. Eric and Ernie would look immaculate (well, when the sketch started they did) and with their old song-and-dance skills still intact, they pulled it off beautifully. And the sets … you

don't see that sort of thing on the telly anymore. Sets like ballrooms. Sets like Fred and Ginger's, like Gene and Donald's.

Ernest Maxin: 'As a child I was in the variety theatre and we used to have a lot of minstrels in the show and I remember I used to see how visual comedy always got bigger laughs than words and so the bigger the set the bigger the visual and the bigger the visual the bigger the laugh.

'Staircases were good because they gave you this idea of vastness. Big, grand staircases descending, they lent it a grace, a style. I tried to bring a touch of Hollywood to it and I don't mean that in a big-headed way. It's just the kind of thing that I loved, so I tried to bring in that gloss, and I think that helped – especially if we were getting laughs at the same time – and that helped to break up the talking in front of the curtain and the sketches. It

brought a touch of the world of make-believe.

'Basically I'm a ham and I love to bring that kind of gloss to the screen. They loved it because Ernie and Eric were Hollywood-mad. We all used to talk about the great Hollywood movies, the world of make-believe and with our limited budget we tried to do the same kind of thing, but always with laughs.

'There was one occasion when Des O'Connor was on the show and they were doing their best to stop him from singing. I had a big staircase made and they were all walking down the stairs and his part of the stairs kept going down and out of sight ...

'Eric was also obsessed with Hollywood, maybe not as much as Ernie, but he still loved it. He loved those big musical numbers, but only as long as there was a good comedy element in it. But Ernie was different. I'm sure when he did *Singin' In The Rain* he really thought he was Gene Kelly in a big

Penelope Keith gets the treatment, Francis Matthews gets the nose

Hollywood studio. Eddie Braben had no input into that part of the show. Eddie was a wonderful dialogue writer for Eric and Ernie. He could put words there – they weren't gags as such but they were so funny because the characters were right for the words and he was marvellous. But all the visual routines, no, he wasn't involved in that side.'

The classic example of this idea was the first sketch that Maxin ever did for Eric and Ernie, the sketch involving Shirley Bassey. She comes on, all glitzed up and like she's overdosed on the glamour pills and starts singing her big Shirley Bassey number. Hair, dress, sequins, chandeliers ... it's all there. In fact, it's so much all there that if you haven't seen the sketch before you think it's for real. After all, that's what Shirley Bassey does. Then she gets her shoe caught in the flooring and it all goes horribly wrong. Eric and Ernie come on – they're wearing workers overalls – and try to get her foot free. They can't. It gets worse and worse. Like the true professional, Bassey just carries on – she will get the song done, and it's the juxtaposition of her professionalism and the mayhem that's going on all around her that makes the gag.

It's the one that always gets repeated. But the other staircase sketch that is often remembered – happily, as it's my favourite – was with Penelope Keith in the 1976 Christmas show.

The scene opens at the top of a staircase. Behind are luscious shimmering curtains, columns lit by candlelight, above are decadent candelabras. At the top of the staircase stands Keith, resplendent in a full-length flowing dress complete with a matching wraparound headscarf. Really, she looks lovely. On one side of her is Eric, on the other Ernie. Both are immaculate in top hat and tails. The scene is perfect. As they start to descend the staircase, the music starts up and they move down each step, high-kicking all the way, Eric and Ernie moving with, if anything, more grace than Penelope, betraying their training as song-and-dance men. If by some chance – if maybe you were a Martian or something – and you'd switched on not knowing that this was *The Morecambe And Wise Show* and that, therefore, something must go wrong, you'd be forgiven for thinking that the scene was entirely kosher.

They dance down maybe ten steps and onto a

landing, kicking and smiling, kicking and smiling and are just about to descend the next ten steps when the camera reveals ... there aren't any more steps. There's just a bit of scaffolding where the steps should be and a sheer drop of maybe eight feet. The music stops. Penelope looks aghast. One by one they clamber down the scaffolding, helping each other and using each other as props to support themselves.

'I can't get down there in this dress,' she says.

'Well, do something with the dress, love,' Eric replies.

Penelope is the last to descend. Her dress rides up. All around her, bits of her dignity lay shattered. They finally straighten themselves up. Penelope's headscarf has partially unfolded so a long piece is hanging down in front of her face. Eric's top hat has one of her golden stilettos stuck in it. As they walk away from the wreckage and towards the camera, Penelope is limping – after all, she's wearing only one high-heeled shoe. Any pretence of grace and grandeur has long departed, except, that is, for Eric and Ernie. They're still trying to carry it off. But it's

too late. The sketch ends with Penelope hitting Ernie around the head with her handbag and limping offstage.

The joy in all this, of course, comes from it being Penelope Keith. Back in 1976 she was one of the biggest stars of the small screen, a real pillar of the tellyocracy. But for all she'd done, she was still best known for – and identified as – the pompous, stuck-up Margot from the hugely popular sit-com *The Good Life*. The Margot character encapsulated everything that was hideous about middle-class, suburban middle England. She was a snob, obsessed with the notion of being correct. Seeing 'Margot' debunked in this way was a joy, both for the audience and for Penelope Keith.

In the public mind, actor and character are so often one and the same. And the better the actor is at acting the part, the more likely this is the case. It's the reason actors are so wary of becoming typecast. Incidentally, we could also talk here about how the public mixed up the stage personas of Eric and Ernie with their real selves, but that's a story for a different time and a different chapter.

Those short, fat, hairy legs in action

I HEAR DES O'CONNOR IS SUFFERING FROM ATHLETE'S VOICE

Eric: 'You mean, people hear his voice and want to run?'

DIANA RIGG, ARTHUR LOWE, John Thaw, Eric Porter ... Shirley Bassey, Tom Jones ... we could fill the rest of the page listing the stars who appeared. Andre Previn. Harold Wilson. Names that a serious production wouldn't be able to get for love nor money lined up, knowing they'd be mocked, insulted and made to look foolish.

The only star ever to back out of the show was the actress Sarah Miles. 'She did go to the rehearsal,' said Ernie, 'but then she said she couldn't go through with it. She was married to the writer Robert Bolt and I think he looked at the

script and told her to get out as quick as she could.'

To go through all the sketches, all the guests ... we'd be here till next week. But Andre Previn, that was a classic. If all the sketches were about was debunking the pomposity of the star and, more importantly, what the star stood for, then it's easy to see why this one stands out. Is there anything more pompous than the world of classical composition? Seeing Eric reduce Grieg's piano concerto to Chopsticks ...

Andre Previn: 'But you're playing all the wrong notes.'

Eric (rising from his piano stool, grabbing Previn by the lapels): 'I'm playing all the right notes, but not necessarily in the right order. I'll give you that, sunshine.'

If we're going to highlight one other person, it has to be Des O'Connor. In 1979, after Eric had had his second heart attack, he received a letter from Des, who said the night before he'd stopped his concert performance half-way through and asked the crowd to pray for Eric Morecambe. Eric replied that it was very kind of Des, but he wasn't sure that those extra sixteen people would make that much difference. That's a story – apparently – but it sums up the Des O'Connor gag. Every week, for years, Des O'Connor would be hugely, hilariously insulted. Sometimes he'd be there, more often he wouldn't – it didn't matter. The gags were there every week.

Eric: 'I blame Eddie Braben for starting the so-called Des O'Connor feud. It was his idea. It was in a 1972 show and we did a sketch where I was a Royal Flying Corps officer in the first world war. The gag was that I answered the phone and Ernie said to me: "I've got some great news." And I said: "What? Has Des O'Connor got a sore throat?"' (The irony of that is that Braben ended up writing scripts for Des in the early 1990s.)

Eric: 'Look, I don't mind him standing here, but I don't want him to sing.'

Ernie: 'But he's here now. We've got to give him something.'

Eric: 'Give him a Get Well Soon card and send him home.'

Ernie: 'Des O'Connor is a self-made man.'

Eric: 'I think it's very good of him to take the blame.'

Des: 'If you don't mind me saying, I'm a famous man. I get recognised in the street.'

Eric: 'So does my dustman. If I see him in the street I say, "There goes my dustman."'

Ernie: 'I hear Des O'Connor is suffering from athlete's voice.'

Eric: 'You mean people hear his voice and want to run?'

Another regular item featured people who would come on for no apparent reason and do nothing, again for no apparent reason.

The first stooge was actress Jenny Lee Wright, who came on and started to take her clothes off as Bo Bo, the striptease dancer. But, curiously, she never got round to completing her routine. Next up was the larger-than-life Janet Webb. A huge woman (49-33-44 for those into numbers), she'd come on at the end of the programme and take the bows, thanking everybody for appearing on her little show. She'd not done anything – she'd not even been on it. It's just that Eric and Ernie thought it would be amusing.

1974 saw the arrival of a new stooge.

'Not now Arthur' became the new catchphrase as mouth-organist Arthur Tolcher came on in his dinner suit and started to play the opening few notes of a tune called the Spanish Gypsy Dance. It never got to be more than a few notes – as soon as he started, either Eric or Ernie would put a sympathetic arm around him and say, 'Not now, Arthur'.

Downcast, Arthur would troop off.

It wasn't, though, the first time Arthur had appeared with Eric and Ernie.

'At the beginning of the war, in 1939, the London Palladium, where I was appearing in *Band Waggon*, closed. When it re-opened, a young song-and-dance man, Ernie Wise, was on the bill to do a show called *Youth Takes A Bow*. And at around the same time, a young Eric Bartholomew came along with his mother and sang a song called I'm Not All There.

But this is the first time in over twenty years I've been available to appear with them since, and I love it.'

THE LINK BETWEEN ANTHEA REDFERN AND ULRIKA JONSSON

We just gave her this dance routine and it made her into the biggest switch-on star overnight – it was enormous.' **ERNEST MAXIN**

A you're Adorable

MAYBE WE SHOULD put this next part in a bit of historical context. Give it a bit of colour. 1977 doesn't sound that far away, but when you start looking at what was happening … it puts things in perspective. Britain was gripped by industrial unrest. Bank rates were running at 14 per cent and the country was in hock to the International Monetary Fund. There were strikes at Heathrow. Bread supplies were hit when drivers refused to deliver to shops which cut prices. There was a blizzard in January and, in time-honoured fashion, it brought the trains to a standstill – it was probably the wrong type of snow. All over the papers, the weather made the headlines; a woman went to make a phone call in a telephone box, and found she couldn't get out because the door had frozen. The Sex Pistols were sacked by EMI and the Rolling Stones' guitarist Keith Richards was convicted for the possession of cocaine. Clive Sinclair began selling his revolutionary two-inch screen television for £175.

There was something else that had the nation buzzing as the New Year kicked off – Angela Rippon's appearance on *The Morecambe And Wise Christmas Show* in 1976. Rippon was an interesting case. OK, so things were starting to get a bit silly on the newsreader front. Suddenly it was very important you had breasts. Angela, Anna … we were only half a mile from the blonde weathergirl. If you want to know the missing televisual link between Anthea Redfern and Ulrika Jonsson, look no further. It was Angela Rippon.

Angela was 'just' a newsreader, but perhaps it was her appearance on the show – more than Glenda Jackson's, more than Shirley Bassey's, more than Laurence Olivier's – that showed how far Eric and Ernie had come.

How it happened …

Ernest Maxin: 'We were working in the studio and we had a lunch break. When I came down the stairs from the control room I saw Angela Rippon standing there and I'm not sure she had an aunt with her or what, but there were two other ladies with her and she said to me, "Ernest, do you mind if I show my aunt and her friend around the studio? They've just come up from Devon."

'Now, I'd seen Angela around in the canteen, but the thing was I'd never seen her legs. I'd only seen her on the news and I'd sometimes sit with her in the canteen, but I was always in and out very quickly and all I ever saw was chest up and this was the first time I'd seen this gorgeous figure. She had this wonderful figure and lovely legs and she had a tight skirt on and she looked absolutely beautiful and I thought to myself, there's something there. So I said, "Do you dance?" And she said, "Yes, I can dance."

'So I went to Eric and Ernie and I said I think we ought to have Angela Rippon on the show. They said to me, "Look, we've had such big film-star names on the show. She's not ready yet. She's a newsreader." I said I thought the element of surprise would be a wonderful gag for the viewers and I said I'd get her to dance but still they weren't keen. I never made them do anything they didn't want to do – that would have been fatal, especially with comedy because you've to be very relaxed in what you're doing. So anyway they said no.

'Two weeks later they were having lunch at Lords cricket ground and Angela Rippon was there and they came back after the lunch – we were actually rehearsing – and they came back and said, "Yes, let's have Angela Rippon on the show", almost as if I hadn't said anything. I don't know what she was wearing, but they must have seen something that was more than just a newsreader.

'I rehearsed with her for several sessions to make sure she would be able to do everything I wanted her to. But she just lifted her leg up and it went round the other side and I just knew then … We just gave her this dance routine and it made her into the biggest switch-on star overnight – it was enormous.'

For Rippon, it marked the watershed of her career. Though a celebrity newsreader, she was still only 34 and, really, how far could this celeb-newsreader thing go? Surely it was only a fad? Wouldn't the men in suits come back? What then? Being invited to do *The Morecambe And Wise Show*, well it was better for your career advancement than even a BA (Hons) from Manchester Polytechnic.

'I was incredibly flattered to be asked to do it. It was, I suppose, the spot to have, the guest spot on *The Morecambe And Wise Christmas Show*. Glenda Jackson had done it, Shirley Bassey … all the big names. I just thought it would be a lot of fun to do, which it was.

'Ernest Maxin rang and asked if I wanted to be in the show. He asked what could I do? Would I like to sing? And I said, "Oh, I don't think so – I'd probably clear the studio" because singing was not my forte, but I did used to dance. I'd never been a professional dancer, but I'd studied classical ballet at a school in Plymouth until I was 17. So I said they might like to think about that, but Ernest said straight away they'd love me to do it. I said the only problem was that they'd have to clear it with TV news, and Alan Protheroe was the editor of TV news at the time, and I said if he gives you the go-ahead, well, that's fine. Alan was quite happy for me to do it. He thought it would be great for me to do it.

'I was slightly anxious because I hadn't actually been dancing for seventeen years, so I went back to my ballet mistress in Plymouth and said look, I've got to get fit for this. I was given plenty of notice so I went back to ballet school for about a month just to get a bit fit again, because sometimes, you know, the spirit is willing but the body is weak. But it was just like riding a bicycle.

'Then Ernest Maxin plotted out what he wanted to do because although I'd said I could dance they'd never actually seen me dance. In the second rehearsal we sort of filled it in a bit, and in the third rehearsal we polished it off. Then we recorded it.

'But it was slightly intimidating because these two men were the most famous men on television and they'd asked me to fill the most important slot on what was, I suppose, the top-rated show of the year, so I was slightly apprehensive about it. But they were lovely to work with, they were such professionals. They knew what they wanted, they knew how to get it, but they made the rehearsal a lot of fun. So it was really as you'd expect – working with absolute pros in any industry. They work hard, but they enjoy what they do and by having that combination they get the best of everybody.'

28, 000, 000 viewers, and no-one won the world cup

Incidentally, Keith Michell, a big, pukka Shakespearean actor, said the same. 'They were so professional, it was an education. The whole event was an education.'

Anyway, back to Angela. 'Ernest Maxin was absolutely wonderful. He was a hoot to work with because he was just like Gene Kelly, you know, everything he does is a kind of dance movement when he's talking and Eric and Ernie used to take the mickey out of him something terrible. But they were both very relaxed in their bodies and very rhythmic. Movement came very easily to them and they were naturally very musical.

'Each of us would suggest something and the thing built and grew as we were doing it and that way of working does give you a wonderful feeling of camaraderie because you are working together as a team.

'They were wonderful hours spent together and they made you feel very comfortable, very much 'you're on the team, you're very important to us' which immediately knocks away any reservations or embarrassments you may have had. So it was just four people working together and having a lot of fun and hoping that what came out of it would be really good.'

In the same show there was another one of the classic plays what Ernie wrote, this time Cyrano De Bergerac. Penelope Keith starred. As ever, there was a killer line:

Eric: 'What do I have to give you for a kiss?'
Penelope: 'Chloroform.'
Waaay-hey!

That show marked the high point of Morecambe and Wise, pulling in twenty-eight million viewers, a staggering number considering no one royal got married, no one landed on the moon and no one won the World Cup. It was just a light entertainment show. And it wasn't the Angela Rippon factor that did that. After all, the viewers had already decided to tune in before she did her bit.

Morecambe and Wise had reached a career crescendo. Twenty-eight million viewers. It was a long way from the Swansea Empire.

THE STRIPPER

I showed it to him, it was about five minutes long, and I could see his face lighten up and he said, "Bloody hell-fire. It works!" And he put his arms around me and gave me a big kiss and a hug and the tears came down his face. He was very emotional, you know, and he kissed me and he started me off. **ERNEST MAXIN**

WITH EVERYTHING THAT'S a legend, there's The Moment – that instant when it crosses the line separating the mortal from the immortal. For most legends it is one thing they do that makes the difference. Cry at Wembley. Invade the Falklands. Tell Gordon Brown that yes, you might be mates, but not about this you're not.

With Eric and Ernie, the moment is harder to pinpoint. Maybe it was when Eric had his first heart attack in 1968. Certainly by the time he had his second in 1979, Eric and Ernie were in their bijou garden flat (which, naturally, they shared) up on Mount Olympus.

Ernest Maxin. You were there. What was that moment? That moment that took these two comics elsewhere?

'A moment? I know what you mean, but I just don't know what to say. There must have been something when we went from seventeen million viewers – which is very popular – to twenty-eight million viewers which is something else entirely. But to be honest, I couldn't tell you what it was.

'Every show we did, it was like the first show you've ever done when there's an audience out there because we all got nervous before a show. In comedy you can't do retakes because if you do you're not going to get a laugh the second time and I never stuck on the canned laughter, I wouldn't. So your heart's in your mouth and you're hoping, hoping, that you haven't made a mistake in your judgement, what should be in and what shouldn't.

'Now with drama, it can be brilliant, very good, good, OK, mediocre, not so good. It's not like that with comedy. With comedy it's either very funny or embarrassing. You have no leeway. Whenever we did a show we were so uptight that all I know

was that from being in the late-teens, ratings wise, we suddenly went into the twenty million and we all felt collectively we had achieved something. I would say what you're talking about happened with the shows they did during the latter years of the BBC before they moved over to Thames. Then I think, that was when it fell away. But, you know, they were offered an enormous salary by Thames. Enormous.'

You want The Moment? I know when it was. It came during Maxin's three-year golden period when they were just untouchable and it was a sketch that described in black and white sounds so … simple, or stupid. There aren't any gags. There are no underlying subtleties, no hidden nuances. No nodding winks to the audience. Nothing.

This is the sketch. Two middle-aged men in their dressing gowns. They've just got up. The relationship? Who knows? Who cares? The sketch starts innocuously enough. They're nosing around the kitchen wondering what to have for breakfast and there's nothing much. So they sit down at the

After The Moment

table and they're listening to the radio and there's a cheap gag about Max Bygraves and ... and nothing. Then the radio announces the next song is going to be The Stripper.

One of them gets up and starts to prepare the breakfast. The other one joins him. It quickly transpires that all their movements, everything they're doing is in time to the music. Grapefruits are cut. Toast pops out of the toaster. Cupboard doors open and close. The fridge opens and closes. All in time to the music. And still, not a word is said between them. That's the sketch.

It's the most bizarre sketch because you just look at it and you think 'What's all that about?' Yet it is probably the most requested and the most repeated Morecambe and Wise sketch there is.

Two men making breakfast in time to The Stripper. It's mad as hell, but there's no one else who could have done it.

Ernest Maxin: 'There were two things, two sketches, that I really enjoyed doing. One was, we were discussing an idea for a kitchen scene and I said, "I'll have something for you tomorrow." They said, "What are you going to do? Some work-out?" And I said, "I don't know but don't worry, I'll have something for you tomorrow", and I went home and I said to my wife, "I can't think of anything. I just can't think of anything." You know, the harder you try to think of something sometimes you just can't. Your mind goes blank. She said, "Well go to bed, get some rest and get up early and do it then." And I said, "No I've got to do it now." So she said, "OK. What do you want for breakfast – toast or grapefruit?" Because sometimes I had a big breakfast, you know and sometimes I had a small breakfast.

'Suddenly I saw the whole routine with cutting the grapefruit and, boing!, the toast popping up and I said "That's it!" and I worked out the routine, going round the kitchen, opening and closing cupboard doors, chopping the grapefruit, mixing the omelette and worked out all the music effects that had to go with that. I made notes and my wife came with me in the car on the way to

work the next morning and I sang it to my wife and wrote the whole thing out long-hand and we worked it all out, you know, which gag came on which beat and then I choreographed it and showed it to them and, of course with their skills and expressions it was much funnier and it worked. We shot that whole thing in fifteen minutes.

'They were marvellous at rehearsing. They really worked so hard. Things like the *Singin' In The Rain* routine. We shot that in about twenty minutes. They worked so hard in rehearsals they never made a mistake in the studio.

'Then, the other thing, and this is where Ernie came to my rescue. I wanted to do this South Pacific number with the newscasters where it looked like they were doing all these acrobatic tricks. I couldn't get them all to rehearse at the same time because they were all on different shift duties and three would come in and then two would come in, and I used to have to stand in for the ones that couldn't come in.

'It was just about two or three days before we were going into the studio, Eric – and he wasn't well at the time, it was his heart condition, you know – Eric said, "This just won't work, Ernest, I cannot see this working." I said, "It will, I promise you. Don't you worry about it. That's my problem."

'He said, "But how will it work technically?" and I explained, but he said, "We've never had them all together." I said, "We'll have them all together when we go into the studio. You just do the same thing you've been doing all the time and the whole thing will fall into place."

'But Eric said, "No. I can't see it. We'll have to do something else." And Ernie said, "Now look, Eric. This is going to work. I'll support Ernest on this. You listen to the two Ernests on this and everything will be all right." And Eric said, "Ernie, I can't see it working." And Ernie said, "You've got to give it a go. We're not doing it live, it's being recorded so we can always cut it out if it doesn't work."

South Pacific Morecambe and Wise style, Christmas 1977: (L-R) Michael Aspel, Philip Jenkinson, Barry Norman, Frank Bough, Eddie Waring, Richard Baker, Richard Whitmore

'So Ernie helped me very much to win him back on that. Anyway, we did it. We went into the studio and shot it in bits and pieces and you could see Eric was a little concerned and wanted to stay back afterwards. What happened was we did the show on the Sunday and this was on the Saturday night. We used to do the musical numbers, record them the day before, so we had the big sets, and then on the Saturday night, before the audience came in, all the sets would be taken out and we'd get the comedy sets in. The next day I edited and stuck together all the musical things that we'd done.

'So Eric said – it was worrying him so much – he said, "Can I come and see the finished edited version?" And I said, "Of course, by all means. Come and watch me do it if you like." He said, "No I'm too edgy. I'll be in the canteen and I'll be walking around. What time do you want me down?" I said what time and he came down and we were just finishing the last shot and he was

white. White. He said, "Well? How's it going? Are we going to put it in tomorrow or what?" I said, "Well, see it now and see what you think." And I showed it to him, it was about five minutes long, and I could see his face lighten up and he said, "Bloody hell-fire. It works!" And he put his arms around me and he gave me a big kiss and a hug and the tears came down his face. He was very emotional, you know, and he kissed me and he started me off.

'When we showed it to the audience – we used to start off at the beginning of the show and when it was time for the musical numbers we would stop and ask the audience to look at the monitors, you know, so we could get the laughter. When we showed it, it literally brought the house down. Angela Rippon was in the control room, she was standing behind me and the laughter in the control room for those of them who hadn't seen the finished thing … You know, the boys were absolutely thrilled.'

WHAT DO YOU THINK OF IT SO FAR?

'You do what you think is funny, what appears funny to you. That's it really.'

JOAN MORECAMBE

PICTURE ERIC MORECAMBE. He's standing on stage in front of a curtain wearing a dinner suit. It's a proper suit, not some joke outfit. Suddenly, he looks directly at the camera – at you – and takes his glasses and moves them a couple of inches so they are askew. Why is that funny?

It's almost impossible to sit down and put into words why something is funny. You can say why something isn't funny. But the thing with humour is that as soon as you try to dissect it, you ruin it.

Ernie: 'My aunt's got a Whistler.'

Eric: 'Now there's a novelty.'

That's funny and it would be in anyone's hands. That was Eddie Braben's talent. In Eric and Ernie's hands, it went from being funny to being a classic. And that was their talent. Eddie himself said: 'If I write a mediocre script they'll make it good. If I write a good script, they'll make it brilliant. One day I might be lucky enough to write a brilliant script and then you'll see something special.' Happily, he did. Every Christmas.

Said Ernie: 'It's hopeless trying to dissect

humour. It's silly really.'

Eric: 'Everybody knows somebody who looks like me or Ern. But it is terrible to start analysing humour. You'd go round the bend. We can make stuff that we've done for years look fresh, that's our strong point. I never know what the public wants. We have standard pillars to work from and we just take it from there.'

Joan Morecambe: 'You do what you think is funny, what appears funny to you. That's it, really.'

It's true. You can only do what you think is funny and hope that everyone else will, too. But Morecambe and Wise had something else. As Eddie Braben said: 'It's not enough to be funny. You also need warmth and affection. Without warmth and affection, you're dead.'

If there's one word to explain Morecambe And Wise's success, it's warmth. They may not have been the funniest comedians ever to tread the boards, and, if we're being honest about it, the humour had a familiar, predictable glow to it. We knew the gags, the catchphrases, the references:

● Ernie had short fat hairy legs.

● And a wig, but you couldn't see the join.

● Eric would cough and say 'Arsenal'.

● Eric would say 'What do you think of it so far?' and then do his stupid ventriloquism – 'ruggish'.

● The two-handed cheek slap.

● Catching an imaginary ball in a paper bag.

● Skewing his glasses.

● Slapping the back of his own neck.

● Asking an off-screen producer, 'Can he say that?' when Ernie used a word he didn't understand.

● Throttling himself behind a curtain.

● The idiot stare at the camera.

● The plays what Ernie wrote.

● References to Luton FC.

● Eric saying 'Pardon?' if Ernie ever made a reference to hearing.

There are probably others and I dare say they'll come to mind later. In one mid-70s show, they highlighted this themselves. Ernie – with his funny haircut where the parting was brushed over from the side, just as if he were going bald – came out in front of the curtain and said: 'You

know, Eric's getting so predictable these days. He does exactly the same things all the time.' He then proceeded to run through exactly what Eric would do: the half-standing behind the curtain pretending he was being strangled, the comments about not being able to see the join on Ernie's wig and the short fat hairy legs, the childlike stare into the camera … And it was all true. As Ernie mentioned the gags, we checked them off in our heads. The gag was that Ernie forgot to mention the slap round the cheeks which – obviously – is what the sketch ended on. But they couldn't have got away with that sketch if it wasn't true. It was a joke, our joke.

Even the big production numbers were all essentially the same. The set would collapse. The guest would be insulted. The sketch would descend into slapstick. But somehow in the world of Morecambe and Wise, it didn't matter. The familiarity bred not contempt, but love.

Eric does the Invisible Man

THE THING ABOUT THE BED

Ernie: 'I remember someone in the BBC hierarchy once commenting on our double bed in some of the sketches. "You can't get into bed together," he said. "You ought to have separate beds." But we thought that would have made it worse. No one else has ever suggested there is anything immoral in it.'
Eric: 'I wear very thick trousers, you see.'

AS MUCH AS THE Glenda Jacksons and the Angela Rippons, it was the 'at home' sketches which endeared Eric and Ernie to the Great British Public.

These, perhaps, were the most curious aspect of Eric and Ernie's shows. Here they were, two middle-aged men living together. Sharing the same lounge, the same breakfast table. Sharing the same bed. Sketches were actually set with them in bed together. Making gags about who was on who's side of the bed. Thinking about it now, it's bizarre ... At the time, though, you just didn't think about it. It wasn't a question of gay or not gay, it was just Eric and Ernie at home and that was that.

And this was on prime-time BBC1. Saturday evening, traditionally the time when all the family got together. To think of the same thing happening now ... There was no knowing nod, no ironic pose. It was an idea that they had 'borrowed' from Laurel and Hardy. Borrowed, but never given back.

Ernie: 'It's great being able to do sketches in that flat without anyone thinking that we might be queer. Mind you, I remember someone in

the BBC hierarchy once commenting on our double bed in some of our sketches. "You can't get into bed together," he said. "You ought to have separate beds." But we thought that would have made it worse. No one else has ever suggested there is anything immoral in it.'

Eric: 'I wear very thick trousers, you see.'

More seriously, Eric said: 'I think we're the only double act, apart from Laurel and Hardy, to share a bed. The audience accepted it from Laurel and Hardy, and now they accept it from us. And it's a great gift.'

Essential to this was the knowledge they felt that way about each other. We knew this because

Christmas 1973 and Diana Rigg dares to come between Eric and Ern

we knew that's how they were. We knew they'd been together since time began, but that really wasn't what convinced us. Eric and Ernie – and Eddie Braben – pulled off the cleverest of all stunts, the subtlest of all manoeuvres. They made us believe the characters we saw on the screen were Morecambe and Wise. It didn't matter they started their show by stepping out, in the grand music-hall tradition, in front of a curtain. It's a supremely clever trick to pull off and it's one that, apart from them, only Woody Allen has managed to do successfully.

We really believed that Eric was a clown, an affable fool, but that somehow he would always be there for Ernie, the small dreamer who fondly spouted his romantic nonsense – 'What are we but empty shells that once were men'. Two idiots, each of whom believed the other to be an idiot, incapable of buying a pint of milk alone. Each looked after the other, and each knew that without them, their partner could not survive.

Eric: 'The essence of our act is that neither of us is the comic and neither is the feed, although it may look that way to the outsider. Put it simply this way. One is an idiot but the other one is a bigger idiot though he tries hard not to show it. One, oozing self-confidence and supposedly slick and worldly-wise, goes along with the idea in order not to deflate his friend whose morale needs a prop, and they finish by sending up the idea which was nonsense anyway.'

The way they personalised themselves added a dimension to their humour that made them more than mere comics. They became human. Eric and Ernie's success in the living rooms of the Great British Public came about simply because we believed in them.

For Eric it proved particularly problematic. Who was he? John Eric Bartholomew or Eric Morecambe? When, in the middle of a sketch, Eric produced a banner saying something daft like 'Luton for the Cup', it was funny because in real life Eric was a director of Luton Town Football Club. Funny for us, but no doubt very confusing for his family.

THEN THE CRACKS STARTED TO APPEAR ...

'If Sir Harold had just walked on without anybody expecting him it would have been a knockout. But everybody was expecting him – the press had broken the story weeks before – and from then on it's just a case of whether he came across better or worse than people expected.'

ERNIE WISE

IN 1978 EVERYTHING, as ever, depended on the Christmas show. And this year, the feeling lurked that it wasn't up to scratch. 'Yes, I've heard the rumours,' Ernie recalled. 'I went out jogging on Boxing Day and someone called out, "Another good one, Ernie. Not quite vintage, perhaps, but … " But I didn't think it was bad. It was another workmanlike Morecambe and Wise show, wasn't it? Anyway, it was the best we could do.'

Of course it was the best they could do. It was always going to be the best they could do. If there was a problem, it was a problem faced by successful artists in every sphere. Expectation. Who was it going to be this year? Who could top last year's Glenda Jackson, last year's Angela Rippon?

'We do try to get to know our audience and we try to anticipate it. When we think they might be expecting something to happen we try to make sure that something else happens … but it's getting more and more difficult.' And so it was with the 1978 Christmas show. For weeks the secret had been out of the bag. It was Sir Harold Wilson. And it wasn't enough. But as Ernie said, 'If Sir Harold had just walked on without anybody expecting him it would have been a knockout. But everybody was expecting him – the press had broken the story weeks before – and from then on it was just a case of whether he came across better or worse than people expected.' Frank Finlay – a big star at the time

It's knees up at Number 10! Sir Harold Wilson's farewell party at Downing Street in 1976: (L-R) Eric, Wilson's sister, Wilson, Lady Marcia Falkender and David Frost

in the drama *Casanova* – wasn't the full shilling. He couldn't relax. He was too tight and it showed. Even Leonard Rossiter didn't work. It was a classic case of being a victim of your own success.

There was more than one problem with the 1978 Christmas show. Eddie Braben, Eric and Ernie's muse, had been left behind at the BBC and had been replaced by John Junkin and Barry Cryer, both of whom, incidentally, had been warm-up men for Morecambe and Wise in another life. Worse, Ernest Maxin was also left back at the BBC. So, crucially, was Eric's health.

The show was too long – seventy-five minutes rather than an hour, and it was bitty and over-produced with too many unnecessary technical tricks and gimmicks. The pace of the show was thrown off balance. Things took too long. Then there were the adverts. The continuity was blown. But it would, everybody agreed, get better.

The next year there was no Christmas show – Eric's heart wasn't in it – but after that the shows carried on. The guests kept coming – in the 1981 Christmas show Sir Ralph Richardson was one of the guests. Playing Disraeli in the sketch, he said: 'No one had served the country with such patriotic fervour than like what I did.' But it wasn't the same. It didn't get better.

Eric and Harold have a bit of a sing-song in 1976

'NO SMOKING OR DRINKING BEFORE 7PM'

'The stress got to him. He got very stressed when it came to our television series, and he found everything more stressful as he got older. I felt it too, but I somehow didn't carry as much responsibility because I just projected Eric. Eric was the end product – he was the one who had to get the laughs, and that was very hard for him.'

ERNIE WISE

THERE WAS A HEAVY price to be paid for stratospheric success. And it looked as if it was Eric who paid it. Certainly, it was Eric who paid in the sense that it was Eric who died. But Ernie, too, paid a heavy price. And some would say the price Ernie had to pay was heavier. We'll get onto that later.

At the beginning of November 1968, Eric Morecambe had a heart attack. It was now they realised just how popular they were. Full houses and good TV ratings are one thing, but the display of public affection shown for Eric took them by surprise.

'We were doing four things at once. We were trying to improve our nightclub act, we were rehearsing for a Royal Command Performance, we were thinking up new material for *The Ed Sullivan Show* and we were preparing a new Christmas show,' said Ernie. 'We'd gone twenty-seven years without ever missing a performance and we both knew that the biggest threat to our work was our health. We'd been telling each other for years to take it easy. We were working at a ridiculous rate – but now this is like stepping off an express train.'

For both partners though, it was a time of

strain, of stress. For Ernie because, for all the bluster and 'the show must go on' talk, it must have been terrifying. If the worst happened, what could he do?

For Eric, the grief option was rather more terminal. 'I was wise-cracking when I came out of hospital after the open-heart surgery. I said things like: "Ernie came visiting. He was in there, making a nuisance of himself walking under the beds". But that was based on fear. If I'd come out looking the way I felt, people would have said, "Not got much time left". After the cameras had gone I sank back and said to Joan, "Didn't do too bad, did I love?".'

It was true that, as Ernie said, 'Eric's health was never good. He never did look terribly well. He had what we call up north a poorly look.' When Eric went down the mines as a Bevan Boy during the war, he was discharged with a weak heart. Smoking between sixty and a hundred cigarettes a day didn't help matters. Still, it was in some ways surprising that it was Eric who got the 'Slow Down' signal. Ernie was the workaholic, the business brain, and Eric said – in all seriousness – that his heart attack was 'God's way of telling Ernie that he needed a rest'.

When Eric had his second heart attack in 1979, there were daily updates regarding his health on the news bulletins. He was referred to as if he were royalty, which in a way he was. The people's royal, loved in a way that a real royal never could be. The day he came out of hospital, it was the lead item. He looked pale and a bit on the wan side, but he was vertical and that was the main thing. The moustache he'd grown ... we won't mention that. Brushes with

mortality can obviously do strange things to a man's mind.

It left both of them floating in a sea of uncertainty. Eric: 'While I am temporarily out of action I can't really expect him to sit around and do nothing. That wouldn't be fair on him. Mind you, he would do nothing if I asked him to, but I know how he enjoys work. If something solo comes up for him, I couldn't expect him to turn it down. If he wanted to do it, he should do it. I certainly wouldn't turn round to him and say "You can't do that". Over the years we have been very loyal to each other. When Ernie rang me recently and we spoke about future plans, I told him that as far as I was concerned, he must do exactly what he wants to do. He said he would do exactly what I wanted him to do, which was marvellous of him.'

Ernie: 'We've had a marvellous ten years since Eric's first heart attack and we must count our blessings. But it would make a lot of sense for us to retire in five years' time. As to what might happen between now and then, I don't think I really want to know.'

Eric put a notice in his living room: 'NO SMOKING OR DRINKING BEFORE 7PM'. 'It also says that my limit is one large scotch and two ounces of tobacco a day. I've had a narrow escape with my second heart attack and it's frightening me. I'm going to be very, very careful. When I wake up every morning, I say to myself, "Take care Eric, you've just had another heart attack." I'm not going to give up my pipe, because I really enjoy it. But I'm cutting down hard on the booze. I know I was drinking too much.'

So how much had Eric been drinking? 'Half a bottle of wine with my lunch, then maybe five large scotches during the evening and chain-smoking cigars at the same time. It just did not make sense for a man with a history of heart trouble.'

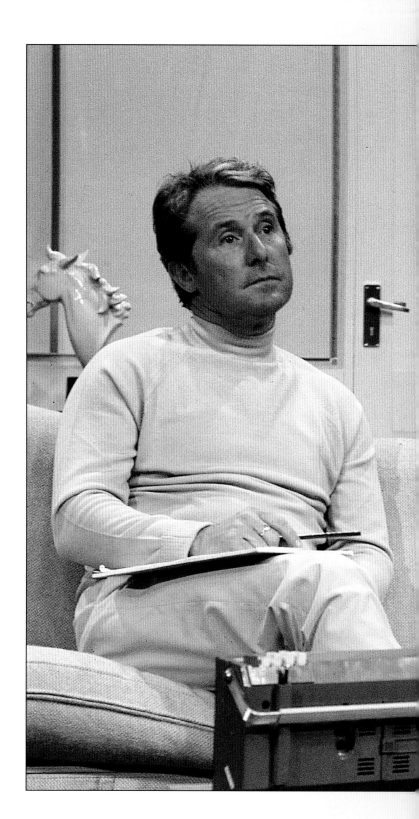

Just another night in for the couple that seemed, somehow, not at all odd

'One is an idiot, the other is a bigger idiot though he tries not to show it. One, self-confident and supposedly worldly wise, goes along with the idea in order not to deflate his friend.'

'And they finish by sending up the idea which was nonsense anyway.'

NOW DO YOU SURRENDER?

'I always think of us as the tortoise and the hare in the old Greek fable. I plod along. I'm an optimist. I get up in the same mood as I went to bed. Frankly, I'm not terribly emotional. Whereas Eric is like the hare. He goes flying off and then takes a rest. He does get excited and emotional and that's the difference between our personalities.'

ERNIE WISE

IT'S THE OLD STORY. It took Ernie seven years to get married. Eric did it in six months. Eric smoked between sixty and a hundred cigarettes a day. Ernie smoked the odd cigar. Eric loved football. Ernie pottered in the garden. Eric burned like a Roman candle. Flaming and colourful. There's only one problem with things like Roman candles: they burn out. And there's nothing that burns out like a comic genius of a roman candle.

Comedians. There's something about the art of comedy that invites stress and tension. We all know the clichés about comedians. How it's a form of warfare. How they say they've murdered the audience when they've done well. Famously, Ken Dodd used to get his audiences rolling and then stand back: 'Now do you surrender?'

Comedians live on the edge in a way that, perhaps, no other type of performer does. An actor goes on stage, he becomes someone else. He says someone else's lines. More often than not, he dresses as someone else. A musician has his instrument to hide behind. Sings a song. Again, it's a part. A comedian, on the other hand … it's naked. And the comic has to do the hardest thing in the world – make people laugh.

Eric had it right when he was talking about the time John Mills was on the show. 'When we started rehearsing for a Colditz sketch, he put on a moustache and then, as the show got nearer, he added a kilt.'

Ernie: 'He was just acquiring a character.'
Eric: 'No he wasn't. He was hiding. Most actors have to hide.'

Barry Took, the comedy scriptwriter and omnipresent TV personality, was a stand-up comic for six years. 'They may have laughed at your jokes a thousand times, but the thousand and first time, they might not. That's what lurks at the back of every comedian's mind. Every time you open your mouth, you're in the firing line. By its very nature, making people laugh is the most difficult job in showbusiness. Every time you tell a joke – or an alleged joke – you either get a laugh or you don't. If you don't, you die. And over the years, that creates a terrible tension.'

It was a tension that ate at Eric. He was the one that had to get the laughs.

As Ernie Wise put it: 'Before you go on stage you can feel the tension just building up and building up. And then you go out and they're all waiting for you and you feel you've just been fired from a gun. Your whole system steps up when you're on stage. All that tension must affect the heart. It is the stage shows in front of live audiences which create the tensions and I think that the important thing when Eric comes out [of hospital] is to take away those pressures, perhaps by concentrating on films.'

It's a telling last line. Eric and Ernie came in for an enormous amount of criticism when they decided to leave the BBC, the BBC which had nurtured them and had made them more than superstars – stratostars? When they joined Thames TV there were cries of 'greed' – and that was from people who were on their side. 'They've got too big for their boots' was typical of the comments. Even Eddie Braben got a bit disillusioned. There's a story that at one stage he got so fed up with being taken for granted he sent them a 'script' of forty blank pages with a note saying, 'If you think writing is so easy, fill in these pages yourselves.'

The British have a curious relationship with the BBC. There are some things they seem to think must be on the BBC. Certain sports events, like Wimbledon and the Boat Race. Things that are institutions. Things that are in the national interest. Morecambe and Wise fell into that category and when word got out that they were taking the shilling and going commercial, well, it hit a nerve.

At the time, Eric and Ernie were quite upfront about their reasons. 'Thames gave us an opportunity to treble our money and we took it,' said Ernie. But there were other motives. Thames made films and Eric and Ernie – especially Ernie – were desperate to make more films. It was, they knew, the only way to Nirvana – America. 'To become international,' said Ernie, 'you have to have the American market. It's all very well to have the British market, but the American market just doesn't accept British products.'

That that was all true is not in doubt. But is it not possible that also lurking at the back of their minds was that the increased wedge from Thames, as well as the chance to make films, was the way to an easier, slower life – a longer life?

'To become international,' said Ernie, 'you have to have the
American market '

THE END

'It does not get any easier. I still expect to see him pop his head around the door. I try not to cry anymore. You can't spend your life crying. I still get lonely. I am lucky to still have family and friends around and there is always someone on the end of the phone who I can speak to. It is simply Eric I am lonely for.' **JOAN MORECAMBE**

ON 28 MAY 1984 Eric Morecambe died. Another heart attack proved too much for a body ravaged by tension and stress. He was just 58.

It's one of the truisms of life that death is hardest on those left behind, but you can't help but feel that in the case of someone like Eric Morecambe, death was actually hardest on him. He had so much more to do, so much more to offer.

After his second heart attack in 1979, he said: 'With so much time on my hands, I want the public to see me grow old. I don't mean I want to retire on a certain date, keep out of view for five years and then make a comeback. I want to keep regularly on the screen and then people won't notice me getting older, they won't notice the change. It's like when your child grows up and you don't notice the change so much because you're there all the time.

'Obviously Ernie and I will continue, but when we do eventually retire I'd like to do something like some character acting. And when I'm, say, 58 or 60 I wouldn't say no to doing something like what Frank Muir does, with a programme like *Call My Bluff*. Frank also does radio and writes books. That's the kind of thing I'd like to do.

'Despite being nudged gently by death twice, I'd still follow the same path if I had my life all over again. I'd do exactly the same, but quicker this time, so that I could retire earlier.'

The real tragedy of Eric's death is that we never got to know the real Eric Morecambe. Eric was an extraordinarily funny man. Everyone you talk to, everything you read, everyone says the same thing. He was hyper-tense, highly emotional, strung tighter than a tennis racquet and occasionally volatile but above all, he was hugely funny.

The thing that comes over about Eric is that he was the worrier, the thinker. He worried about the show, getting laughs, his health – everything. It's a curious thing but of the two, Eric was the family man (they were both happily married, but Eric was the one with the kids. The Morecambes loved children. After having two of their own, they decided to adopt a third. Ernie and Doreen had no children) and that implies a certain stability. And he was stable, though in a volatile way. In addition he was incredibly well read, erudite and had a wonderful turn of phrase. Here's what he wrote about their breakthrough year in *Eric & Ernie* (with Dennis Holman):

'1964 bounded in leaving us breathless, intoxicated. Whatever we touched turned to gold and money was pouring in. Wasn't that what we'd been striving for all these years? Only it seemed that the problem with making big money was that it became a habit. You couldn't refuse anything. After the tough early times and all the years of struggle, you hate turning anything down. You become like Pavlov's Dog except instead of salivating when the bell goes, your hand goes involuntarily into the signing twitch.

'So it began, the treadmill to Oblivion. It was the plodding round of show after show after show. Before each the pleasurable anticipation, then the fears, the returning insecurity – will they reject us? The rituals of make-up and superstition. The familiar dressing-room smells, the pinpricks of discomfort, the butterflies in the stomach, the tributes, the deferences, the knock on the door. That bladder again though you know it will only be a few drops, a nuisance to be shaken off. The ascent into the wings. The girls on the brightly lit stage garish in close-up, damp with sweat as they crowd past you. The darkened audience – what

'**When we do eventually retire I'd like to do something like character acting.**

'**And when I'm 60 I wouldn't say no to doing something like Frank Muir does on Call My Bluff ...**'

A year after Eric's death, Ernie went on a five-week song and
dance tour of Australia. It was what he did

are they like tonight? The drum roll, then suddenly you're on and you're no longer yourself but an addict in an adrenaline fix that takes you through an hour and a quarter of a sort of unendurable pleasure, indefinitely prolonged to a climax of final applause and a detumescence that leaves you sweating and shaking, clear-headed about every detail of the performance, but curiously numb to all else. People are talking. Drinks being offered. Bustle. Sounds. Faces. People, people. Doors shutting so loud they hurt. Then you're limp, sitting in a chair, peeling off your wet clothes, slugging back a drink, dragging on a cigarette …

'This is success. This is what you've stalked and captured, the triumph of successful suffering, this spasm of creativity but not the creativity of something finite like a building or a state but a creativity so much more lasting because you have fixed in time a moment of satisfaction for a polyglot entity called an audience, participated in it, and centred their attention upon yourself which is something on which you are hooked.'

It's a wonderful passage, full of colours and smells and tastes, and it displayed the workings of a brain that could do something a little more creative than catch an imaginary pebble in a brown paper bag.

The family aside, Eric's two hobbies were bird-spotting and fishing, two of the most peaceful pastimes you could ever find. Eric didn't eat fish, and somehow that seems the way it should be.

Apart from writing the autobiography (*Eric & Ernie, The autobiography of Morecambe & Wise* published in 1972), and contributing to various other books about Morecambe and Wise, Eric wrote a novel, *Mr Lonely* (not as maudlin as it sounds), two children's stories, *The Reluctant Vampire* and *The Vampire's Revenge*, and the posthumously published *Eric Morecambe On Fishing*. The idea that he may have turned into a mature radio wit spilling out with anecdotes and stories is just too sad to contemplate.

Joan said, 'It does not get any easier. I still expect to

see him pop his head around the door. I try not to cry anymore. You can't spend your life crying. I still get lonely. I am lucky to still have family and friend around and there is always someone on the end of the phone who I can speak to. It is simply Eric that I am lonely for.'

Anyone who has ever lost someone close to them – and, one way or another, that's just about everybody – will know exactly what Joan means. The idea that someone has gone, that you'll never ever see that face again, you'll never hear that voice, smell that smell... somehow it seems unnatural. When that person is still on TV practically every week, it must be a very strange feeling indeed.

'I still see myself as married to Eric. I still wear his ring and feel I will be his wife until the day I die.' Unlike Tommy Cooper's wife Gwen, who found out after his death that he'd been having an affair for seventeen years, Joan found no skeletons. 'We had a very good relationship and a very good marriage. I'm sure it never crossed Eric's mind to be unfaithful just as it never crossed mine. We both took marriage very seriously. I'm sure there were great temptations when he was working away - there are bound to be in showbusiness. But he would never have contemplated doing the dirty on me.'

In the years since his death, BBC repeats aside, most of the noise about Eric has come from his son, Gary. It transpires that Eric was not the perfect dad. 'Eric was not a difficult or hard parent,' says Gary, 'He was soft and silly for 90% of the time, and unpredictable for the rest. If anything he allowed us too much freedom, because the idea of being a hands-on parent horrified him. He was understandably much happier getting on with what he was best at, and leaving the domestic stuff to my mother.'

In his book, Eric Morecambe Behind The Sunshine, Gary did a bit of kiss and telling and well. . . you make your bed. All of which would be of marginal interest, but growing up with a famous dad, someone like Eric Morecambe, of course the kids are going to complain.

I can remember going shopping with my dad and being absurdly embarrassed by him playing around, chatting with the sales staff, joking with anyone who'd listen. Why couldn't he be like all those other dads? Quiet, anonymous and not so blimmin' embarrassing.

But time passes and now I'm in his position and the story's the same, only I'm on the receiving end.

It is, I'm sure, an experience that everyone's had and that, really, is the only reason I bring it up here.

Ernie: 'What's the matter?' Eric: 'It's that reindeer at the back –
his nose is freezing.' Ernie: 'That's Rudolph, he's got a red nose.'
Eric: 'He'll have a black eye if he does that again.' (Christmas 72)

At home in Harpenden with Joan and Gary

'We had a very good
marriage. I'm sure it never
crossed Eric's mind to be
unfaithful ... he would never
have contemplated doing the
dirty on me.'

'He often pretended to stab himself with his knife and drop dead at the table. Other diners would stare at us or - worse - pretend not to. "Stop it dad," I would beg him.'

'I dreaded going out to restaurants with him because he could never just sit there and have a quiet meal like an ordinary dad. He often clowned around with the waiters, pretending to stab himself with a knife and drop dead on the table, or else sip at an empty glass and exclaim: "The wine is superb!" The other diners would stare at us or – worse – pretend not to. "Stop it, dad! Stop it," I would beg him.'

Can you imagine what it must have been like growing up as Gary Morecambe, Eric's son? He's never there, working all the hours God sends, the stress is driving him mad and turning him into a nicotine junkie, and every time he goes out, it's all – 'Go on, tell us a joke. Be funny. You're funny. Go on then, be funny.'

'He'd talk very loudly and crack jokes with everyone, whether they be shop assistants, passers by or shop-vendors. Fans would ask for his autograph and he always gave it, handing it back with a flourish and the throw-away line: "Just take this prescription to Boots The Chemist."'

So wrote Gary in *Eric Morecambe Behind The Sunshine*, which was published in 1994. So what did he want? A manic-depressive alcoholic? Look, Gary, he left you with enough material to write a book and a play. So he wasn't there much and he was an egomaniac. It goes with the territory of being a public figure, a performer. Just like writing books that proclaim, 'Dad made the world laugh. So why did he make my childhood a misery?' comes with the territory of being the offspring of such a performer.

Without wanting to sound too unsympathetic, you can't help but feel that Gary got off lightly. Most kids in his situation would have ended up in the Betty Ford Clinic, afraid to walk past a magnet for fear their nose might be drawn unnaturally to it. Showbiz kids, just making movies of themselves, I guess.

Eric's ashes are kept in a little urn – it had to be, really – in a small church near his home in Hertfordshire. Next to his name in the records book, someone has drawn a small pair of distinctive glasses. 'They were his trademark,' said Joan. 'I found it rather moving.'

'Britannia Airways is to name its new Boeing 757 after the comedian Eric Morecambe, it was announced today.'
The Sunday Telegraph, 16 April 1995

Eric would have liked that. Idiot nonsense.

'... And then I did this really funny gag where I pretended to stab myself with my knife – the waiters were killing themselves...'

'I was wise-cracking when I came out of hospital after the open-heart surgery. I said things like: "Ernie came visiting. He was in there, making a nuisance of himself walking under the beds". But that was based on fear...

...If I'd come out looking the way I felt, people would have said, "Not got much time left". After the cameras had gone I sank back and said to Joan, "Didn't do too bad, did I love?"'

STILL ON MY WAY TO CRICKL ... HOLLYWOOD

'I still need that high from performing and I still need to prove something. I want to do it. No, I need to do it.'

ERNIE WISE

IN 1985, ERNIE went back to work. Not so strange. As he said, 'I've worked hard since I was 10 years old and I don't like being a casual worker. I like to be employed. I don't want to retire and put my feet up. If I haven't got any purpose in life, I'm lost.' It's a standard line from a working-class workaholic. The work that he chose to do, though – that wasn't standard.

Just over a year after Eric died, he set off on a five-week tour of Australia, a song and dance show. On the face of it, what a very strange thing to do. Australia. It's true that Morecambe and Wise went down very well there, and that, at heart, Ernie was a song-and-dance man. And it's true going to Australia had a certain logic. After all, if he'd done it in England, it would have been Eric this and Eric that and he wouldn't have been taken at face value, as Ernie Wise, the song-and-dance man. All of those things we accept, and yet ... Still, what a very strange thing to do.

This is a 60-year-old man, with a swimming pool and a tennis court and a boat moored outside his huge house overlooking the Thames. This is a man with a Roller whose personalised number plate reads ERNIE. This man does not need to go to work, working-class ethic or no working-class ethic. Going to Australia on a five-week tour? They breed them tough in Yorkshire.

In February 1985, Ernie found himself in Hollywood, fulfilling a dream. He'd always wanted to go there but Eric, a notoriously bad traveller, wasn't up for it. Every time Ernie, the

John Thaw and Dennis Waterman in uniform for once, for the Christmas special, 1976

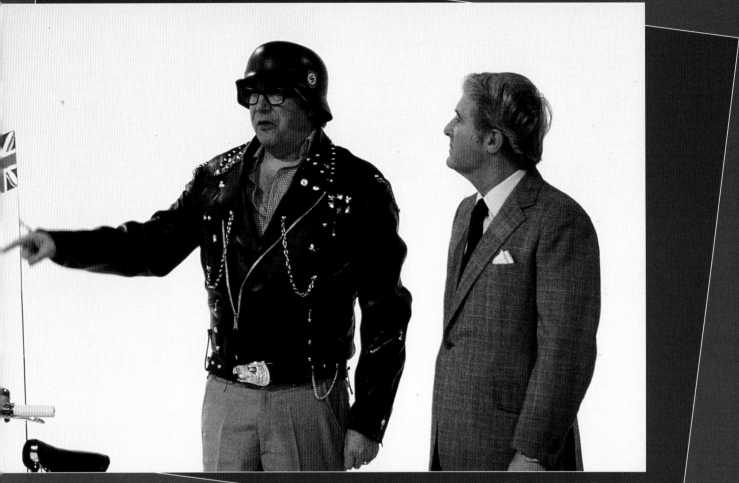

Eric as a Hell's Grandad

romantic dreamer, went off on a flight of fancy about Hollywood, Eric would rabbit on about Cricklewood.

Some friends at Thames Television arranged for him to have a guest role in the American sit-com *Too Close For Comfort*, which starred Ted Knight, a comic actor who'd made his name in the ground-breaking *Mary Tyler Moore Show*. 'I think I can cope, though it's very frightening in a way. I've never done situation comedy.' The Hollywood fantasy thing was true, though – 'I've always had this fantasy about Hollywood, it started when I was a kid watching Mickey Rooney in the cinema. I had a dream that one day I would go to Hollywood. That was one of my ambitions and now it's coming true. I love the place. It's so exciting.' Again, it's no coincidence that he went to work outside Britain. Breaking free is never easy and to the Great British Public, Ernie Wise was only ever going to be one half of a whole.

'After Eric died, I decided to stay in show-business because I wanted to be wanted. I think that's the real answer. I don't have to worry about money, but I just need enough work to keep me ticking over. To stay alive. I am in my sixtieth year and this is my first appearance in Hollywood. If they ask me to do something else, I'll be very happy, but if they don't want me, I'll still be happy.' Just as well, because they didn't.

Two years later, he made another odd choice. He chose to appear in a West End musical, *The Mystery Of Edwin Drood*. The last time he'd done the West End was in 1939 with Arthur Askey's *Band Waggon*. Without wanting to get too Sigmund about all this, what was this man trying to escape?

IF ERIC WAS BRITAIN'S BEST-LOVED COMIC, WHAT DID THAT MAKE ERNIE?

'Ernie wasn't a victim. He was a professional gifted with the timing of a district nurse, but it's a skill that has been all but lost with the ascendancy of television.'

THERE'S A STORY that after Eric suffered the second of his two heart attacks, Ernie was so fed up with people coming up to him and asking how Eric was that he had a badge made: 'Eric is much better, thank you. But I don't feel too good.'

It was trawling the Internet that gave the most graphic insight into the role of Ernie Wise in the Great British Institution known as Morecambe and Wise. It might seem a curious place to look, but in equally curious way, it made perfect sense to look there. It would, so the theory goes, give a useful window on how the new viewed the old, how the future saw the past.

There was only one web site that discussed Morecambe and Wise. This isn't so surprising – after all, Morecambe and Wise are as locked in the old world as the Internet is in the new. But this site threw the sharpest of lights on the modern view of Ernie Wise.

The entry for Eric Morecambe went on for a number of pages: 'On 14 May 1926, John Eric Bartholomew was born to parents George and Sadie. He was later to become known as Eric Morecambe, and to bring joy to the lives of millions as half of Britain's best-loved comedy act ...' And on it went, talking about 'Britain's best-loved comic' with a fondness and affection that, despite the fact its subject died thirteen years ago and was probably written by someone who isn't even old enough to have seen the repeats, was very real and very touching.

Kings of Comedy, Christmas 1973

The entry for Ernie was this: 'On 27 November 1925, Ernest Wiseman was born to parents Harry and Connie.' And that's it. No biography, no life story, no pen portraits. And no references to being anyone's best-loved comic. Oh, there's a reference to the page being incomplete and that there is 'more to come', but let's be realistic here. Ernie's getting on. There isn't more to come. Well, not much anyway.

Eric and Ernie were together for forty-six years and always, always, it was Eric who was the funny one, Eric who got the attention. What must it have been like? Being in a partnership and always taking the back seat and, more importantly, always being perceived as taking the back seat.

When people talk about comedy duos, they always make the analogy of a marriage, but that's wrong. Marriage is at its best a loving relationship, at its worst a working partnership. Showbusiness comedy duos are similar in many respects but they differ in one vital way. Both partners are, in the nicest possible way, egomaniacs. Show-offs. They've got to be – they wouldn't be in the business otherwise.

If, in a marriage, one of the partners gets overlooked – typically the wife who doesn't 'work' – then it's not a good thing, but it stops somewhere short of being terrible. The overlooked partner did not go into the marriage with the avowed aim of receiving adulation. They don't have that ravenous ego to deal with.

How must it have been for Ernie Wise?

But there's another reason why showbusiness duos – and specifically comedy duos – are different to married couples, and it's a reason that's in the very nature of comedy. It's the fool that triumphs, that's why it's funny, and in a duo where one partner is the fool and the other is straight and sensible, well, it doesn't take much to work out where the sympathy is going to go. (How often is it that the stay-at-home spouse is, in truth, the straight, sensible one while the wage earner is the one who goes out and lightens up?)

All these rationalisations for something that's really quite straightforward. Eric Morecambe was Britain's best-loved comic. It's not something that's in doubt and it's probably just as true now as it was in 1984 when he died, as it was in the mid-70s when he was at his peak. But the question remains. If Eric was Britain's best-loved comic, what did that make Ernie? Again, the answer is quite straightforward. Ernie Wise was Eric Morecambe's best-loved comic. And if he wasn't, he should have been. For without Ernie, there wouldn't have been an Eric.

Ernie's consummate skill was as a straight man. He wasn't a stooge, there's something about that word that implies victim. And Ernie wasn't a victim. He was a professional gifted with the timing of a district nurse, but it's a skill that's been all but lost with the advent and ascendancy of television. Television killed off the straight man in a way it never did the funny man because its multi-camera angles and pre-recorded links and editing suites did away with the need for pin-sharp timing. You still needed the clown, the upfront comic genius, but the subtleties? You could edit them in afterwards.

The straight man is all about leaving gaps and spaces for the funny man to perform into. It's a very intimate art, full of subtle nuances, small gestures and silent movements. It's the funny man who does the big movements, the verbal and physical slapstick. One counterbalances the other. It's a question of harmony. You cannot have two people being loud, just as you can't have two people being soft. It's the way the world is set up – the yin and the yang.

Take, for example, a quite routine sketch they did. Out walked Ernie looking for all the world like a tennis player. Proper tennis shoes, socks, short shorts, white sweater and proper racquet. He'd kept himself in trim and he looked like someone you'd see in a reasonably well-off, middle-class, suburban tennis club. We, the audience, laughed, not because of anything that Ernie had done but, as is so often the case, out of sheer anticipation. Ernie looked so proper, we just knew that Eric would be, well, Eric. And he didn't disappoint. Black shoes, grey socks held up by sock suspenders, ridiculously baggy shorts, the hems of which were lined with wire so as to make them appear as wide as possible, an ill-fitting shirt and a neat white headband that looked absurd on his balding head. His racquet, needless to say, looked Victorian.

Eric would have looked funny regardless, but it was the contrast with the immaculate Ernie that made the joke something more than straight slapstick. Ernie didn't look funny at all. Not by himself, not with Eric. Not funny. But he needed to be there. And if he hadn't been there, Eric would have been ordinary. Just another clown.

WHAT WERE THEY REALLY LIKE?

'As long as there's a cinema celluloid screen there will always be a Laurel and Hardy, and as long as there's an electronic television screen there will always be Morecambe and Wise.' **ERNEST MAXIN**

THERE ARE TWO essential questions which remain: 'How close were the real Eric and Ernie to their on-screen characters', and 'Could that level of popularity happen again'.

For the first question, it's probably wise to ask some of those who knew them best.

Ernest Maxin: 'Well, Eric was exactly the same as you saw him. He was a very funny man. Ernie, if you watch the shows now, was a great comedian in his own right. I used to give him more funny things to do, and in his dialogue he was brilliant. The difference was that Eric was a funny comedian and Ernie was a comedy actor and the combination of the two was absolutely wonderful. Looking at the repeats of the shows now, Ernie gets enormous laughs. And they were lovely fellas.

'Eric was very on edge and Ernie was a calming influence on him. Eric was very emotional. There were times when, if I wanted to tell Eric something, I'd think, well I won't tell him now.'

Was he hot-tempered? 'No. I wouldn't tell him because, let's say he was worried about something in the show at rehearsals, If I brought it up when I knew he was worried it would get worse because he would get nervous about it and want to put his point of view and he'd get very excited. He was very funny at rehearsals, Eric, and he had me in hysterics most of the time, but I would wait until one of those moments came along when he would make me laugh and I'd say something that would make him laugh, then I could bring it up. Then we would talk and that was fine.'

Angela Rippon: 'There was a greater depth to them than you saw. Eric was compulsively funny. He couldn't stop himself from being funny, but there was a depth to him and you'd be having quite a serious conversation with him about something and then ... suddenly he'd put his glasses on sideways or something and he'd snap out of it. He couldn't help it. It was almost as if he felt he had to put a punctuation point in there somewhere and then he'd snap back into being serious again.

'He was a very kind man, and Ernie similarly. There's a lot more to him than just the straight man in the partnership. One was absolutely necessary to the other. It was like a piece of scaffolding. If you took one away, the other wouldn't necessarily stand on its own. They were the perfect partnership. Their sense of humour was the same ... they just meshed, like Siamese twins.

'Ernie was always ever so slightly quieter, but still he was coming out with his sharp one-liners. And even now, though he's not very well, Ernie will still perform for his public because he knows that's what people expect of him. Privately, one to one, having lunch or dinner with him, he's just great company, a great traveller. Someone who loves showbusiness and loves talking about it and loves to be part of it. And they've both got smashing wives, lovely people who've both got their feet firmly on the ground.

'Probably the most interesting thing about them was that they never got grand. That is the nice thing about them. They were always the same with

'Genuinely, I never saw them have an argument. There was so much respect on both sides; more than anything, they needed each other.'

The nation's favourite puppetmaster, Harry Corbett, meets the nation's favourite comics. Sooty came too, January 1973

everybody. If they saw people in the street, it was never too much trouble to turn on a little bit of the act. They were of the old school. They knew what people wanted. They'd spent too many years trying to win the audience over to want to let them go once they had them. And also they had that old-school mentality that said they also had a responsibility to their audience. The audience put them there, the audience could take them away.'

Johnny Speight: 'Eric was a truly funny man. You just laughed at him as he walked in the room. He was always coming up with ideas. Eric was a natural for television. His expressions just came naturally. He was a good dancer and mover and he could do a wonderful fall – the best of any comic I have ever seen.'

There's another question, this one a touch sensitive. Did Ernie ever get jealous of Eric, because of all the attention he got?

Maxin: 'No, I never saw anything like that. You've got to remember, they were in business and they both knew how they were, this was the right thing. Laurel and Hardy were funny in their own way, but it was only the contrast. No, I never saw that happen at all. They'd been at it for so many years so if there were any feelings like that on either side it would have come out then or soon after. Genuinely, I never saw them have an argument. There was so much respect on both sides, but more than anything, they both needed each other. They were clever enough to know they were both as important as each other.'

Rippon: 'No, not at all. Neither of them had an ego that said, "Morecambe and Wise are pretty good, but I can go off and make it on my own." They were both very astute businessmen. And you can take every adage in the book, but basically they knew the truth: if it ain't broke, don't fix it.

'There was something very special about the two of them. They recognised that in each other and it was a sign of their generosity, because one never felt he was more important than the other or that he could make it on his own.

'They had an act that worked and they were both astute enough to realise that Morecambe and Wise as a team were going to be the biggest thing on British television this century. Morecambe on his own, Wise on his own would be just two other comedians. Together they were a comic phenomenon. There was nobody and there has not been anybody to touch them. Now, how stupid if they had thrown all of that away for individual glory. They didn't need that. It comes back to that combination of having brilliant business sense, perfect comic timing and a generosity of spirit. They were special as comics, they were special as businessmen, and they were special as human beings.'

Were they easy to be friends with?

Maxin: 'I was very close with both Eric and Ernie … Socially we didn't meet, only on certain occasions when it concerned the show, but we were very close when we were working. I mean, look, we're all men, but we used to kiss each other with emotional love and when I talk about Eric now I get a little lump in the throat. I think in a way they loved me too. I think knowing I had this feeling for them, that I was on their side, I think they respected me and they certainly showed me a lot of affection. More than anyone else I've worked with.'

Rippon: 'I got very close to them and their families

and we've kept in touch. I still see them socially and I think that that is the measure of them as people. They didn't just pick you up and drop you. It wasn't a question of, "Oh, we need you on our programme", and after that you're just a name on the credits. It wasn't that. Warmth is the perfect word to use because there was a genuine friendliness about them.

'Constantly making comparisons with people now isn't the right way to do it because they were of their time and not this. They had a different set of values and a different way of doing things and a different attitude towards showbusiness life. They weren't showbiz, they were performers, they were pros. They weren't glitzy and they never gave themselves airs and graces. I think that came across in their performance and their private lives.'

Another question. Were they friends? Did they like each other? Maxin: 'They didn't see each other as far as I knew. I think one of the reasons for their longevity was that when their work was finished, they used to go their separate ways. I don't think they socialised together at all and I think that was why it was always fresh when they came into rehearsals. They never took it home with them.'

After all, Eric and Ernie had been living in each other's pockets since their mid-teens. They'd lived together, married women from the same background, bought exactly the same cars, houses in exactly the same areas ... They didn't need to see each other, too.

Eric: 'We avoid each other socially as a general rule unless we have to go out together. But normally we only see each other when we are working. And maybe that's not the best time to be together because we are both often under quite a bit of pressure. Things can get rather heated when we are writing or rehearsing, especially when one of us feels that the other one is

Agent 003.5 and
Superman's Uncle

doing something wrong. At social events, attended by either of us, people often ask where the other is and it's hard to explain. All I can say is that ours is a relationship where we both know where to draw the line. Anyway, Ernie lives a different kind of life. He's a non-family man.'

Ernie and Doreen decided against having children – they felt it was incompatible with life on the road. Ernie wasn't a one for a big social whirl. Most of his friends, though, came from the same place that he had – the music hall. Pearl Carr and Teddy Johnson, Harry Worth, Norman Vaughan … these were the people in the Wise inner circle. 'We've been through all the same things together. We all used to tour together and we've been through the same digs – Mrs Coombs in Birmingham, Mrs Mackay, 11 Daisy Avenue in Manchester. It's like a fraternity. We all know each other's way of life.'

As to the last question, could it happen now? No, it won't happen again. Society is not as homogeneous. Technology has ensured there will never again be that same mass experience – or at least not for something like a light entertainment show.

'I don't think that we will ever see the likes of Morecambe and Wise again,' said Eddie Braben. 'Their programmes were very expensive to make, and the BBC won't spend the cash. Instead they are producing quiz shows and one unfunny situation comedy after another simply because they are cheap.'

Ernest Maxin: 'It could happen now if there was somebody doing it. I thought they were marvellous and there hasn't been anyone else like them. And there is a reason for this. You see, Eric and Ernie learned from other people when they were young and apart from learning what to do, they learnt what not to do. Other people told you, people who were more experienced than you.

'But youngsters today, it doesn't happen. In those days, you worked in the theatres and you got to know different audiences and you learnt how to pace yourself, how to work the audience. And remember, Eric and Ernie were clean. No era has cleverer or more talented people than any other, but they had a wonderful schooling in playing all the wonderful theatres and all the terrible theatres.

'And another thing I shall say, which I suppose I shouldn't, is that you wouldn't go to a surgeon and have an operation if he hadn't been a medical student first. During the time when I was learning about television, all the people in the top positions, the controllers of programmes, the head of comedy, the head of drama or whatever, they'd all been either actors, entertainers, performers or maybe producers in the theatre. They'd learnt their trade and that was the position they'd acquired so they could pass down their knowledge to you.

'I'm not saying that the people were any cleverer then, but now the people in those positions just don't have that experience.'

The answer's no, then.

One of a kind. It won't happen again

Ernie and Doreen

Eric and Joan

Mad as hell. But it worked

PARDON?

In 1994, the BBC made a tribute programme to Morecambe and Wise. They didn't ask Ernie to participate because they 'didn't want too many talking heads'.

ERIC DIED YOUNG – 58 is no age. He worked hard as nails all his life, fretting, worrying, dragging his guts around the country. Working, sweating, working, until one day, he made it. He reached the top and then just when it was time to enjoy it, to do maybe a bit of what Frank Muir does, he had it taken away. Really, it's terrible. Maybe worse, though, was Ernie's fate. He lived to see it go. Slowly but surely, his fame was taken away from him. In Eric's life Ernie was overshadowed; in his death he wasn't even that.

In 1978, the Birmingham branch of the Variety Club arranged a dinner in honour of Morecambe and Wise. A big black-tie do with all the usual British showbiz suspects. ATV decided to televise it. But the thing was, the dinner was over four hours long and the programme was only going to be half an hour. So they cut out Ernie Wise. 'What a blow to the old ego,' he said afterwards. 'I'm not being big-headed about this, but I thought the whole thing was supposed to be a tribute to us, and I had taken a lot of trouble over that speech. I know that things get cut – we've done it ourselves on occasion – but I feel that on this occasion they could have kept in just a snippet of my speech.' It doesn't need to be said, but they didn't cut Eric's bit.

In 1994, the BBC decided to make a big television tribute to those lovable comedians Morecambe. 'It's news to me,' said Ernie from his home in Berkshire. 'I have not been approached.' The BBC found time to ask John Thaw, Glenda Jackson, Cliff Richard. They found time to get Ben Elton. But they didn't have the time to ask Ernie Wise. Maybe he had moved and hadn't forwarded his address.

'I do find it odd,' said Ernie. 'You would think they'd ask for my memories.' A BBC spokesman said, 'We did not want too many talking heads.'

That's lovely. The BBC makes a tribute programme to Morecambe and Wise but doesn't ask Ernie. You can't

Ernie was never a stooge, he was the best straight man in the business. Without Ernie there wouldn't have been an Eric

help but feel that, if only he was happy, then that would be OK. But from the little we know about him, it doesn't seem that way. In 1988, he got hot and bothered because Citroën had used his name in one of their car ads. Though completely innocuous, the line, 'It's the Wise way to travel to Morecambe', made Ernie 'very, very upset'. A year later, he described himself as 'a showbiz outcast', complaining: 'In the old days the phone never stopped ringing. But those days are over. I just don't have the clout anymore.' The sad thing is, it's true.

Ernie Wise was a hugely talented entertainer. He was a song-and-dance man, a comedian and a comic actor. He was also the best straight man Britain has ever produced. But he chose to work with a genuine comic genius and that was both his blessing and his curse.

Everything he did was overshadowed by Eric. Not because of the act, not because of their peers, but because of you and me, their public. Ernie could come on stage and do the best routine in the world and it would be top entertainment. But then Eric would walk on the stage, say nothing and move his glasses maybe two inches to the side of his nose and Ernie would disappear. On his own, Ernie Wise would have been a very good, maybe a great performer. Eric Morecambe took him somewhere else entirely. And no one would ever let him forget that.

In 1995, on his 70th birthday and after more than sixty years in showbusiness, Ernie Wise announced his retirement. It was eleven years after Eric's death. In many ways, Ernie was just making it official. But it's highly unlikely he would see it that way.

'I'd like to have gone on forever. A lot of people told me they thought I would.' But no one goes on forever. In December 1993, he suffered a stroke. 'Once I had the stroke I realised I was finished.' A second stroke, in August 1995, took away any confusion that might have still been lurking within the driven showbiz soul. It was time to say, 'Ladies and gentlemen, thank you and goodnight.'

'My eyesight is going and my hearing is not very good,' said Ernie.

Pardon?

Picture credits:

Cover: Thames Television Ltd, a Pearson Television company
BBC: pages 25, 51, 55, 56, 57, 58/59, 62, 63, 69, 74, 79, 80/81, 91, 96/97, 101, 105, 112/113
Camera Press: page 66
Camera Press/Joe Balaitis: pages 76, 77
Camera Press/Gianni Dalla Pozza: page 64
Camera Press/David Gaywood: page 120
Camera Press/Dimitri Kasterine: page 82
Camera Press/Ian Swift: page 88
Mander & Mitchenson: pages 36, 46, 47
The Moviestore Collection: pages 38, 39
Pictorial Press: pages 13, 17, 19, 20, 21, 26, 28/29, 30, 32/33, 36, 43, 44
Rex Features/Ian Jeayes: pages 41, 53
Rex Features: pages 40, 41, 70, 119, 121
Ronald Grant Archives: pages 14, 15, 60
Scope Features: pages 5, 6, 8, 49, 71, 87, 92, 93, 95, 99
Thames Televsion Ltd: pages 61, 67, 72/73, 85, 102, 108, 111, 116, 122, 124, 127

Video covers on page 128 reproduced by kind permission of 4 Front Video

Picture research: Odile Schmitz

BIBLIOGRAPHY

Eric And Ernie – The autobiography of Morecambe & Wise
with Dennis Holman (*WH Allen, 1972*)

The Best Of Morecambe And Wise
by Eddie Braben (*The Woburn Press, 1974*)

The Morecambe And Wise Special
(*Weidenfield & Nicholson, 1977*)

Bring Me Laughter
by Bruce Crowther and Mike Pinfold
(*Columbus Books, 1987*)

Still On My Way To Hollywood
by Ernie Wise (*Isis Audio Books, 1992*)

Eric Morecambe Behind The Sunshine
by Gary Morecambe and Martin Sterling
(*Robson Books, 1994*)

Classic British TV
(*Guinness Publishing*)

Newspapers:
The Daily Express
The Daily Mail
The Daily Mail Weekend
The Daily Mirror
The Daily Star
The Daily Telegraph
The Financial Times
The Independent
The Morning Star
The Observer
The Sun
The Sunday Express
The Sunday People
The Sunday Telegraph
The Sunday Telegraph Magazine
The Sunday Times
The Times
Today

…and about a thousand tapes of TV programmes.